I0020033

Chatgpt

A Guide to Making Money With Chatgpt

(Creative Ways for Teens and Young Adults to Make Money With Chatgpt)

Thomas Trotter

Published By **Elena Holly**

Thomas Trotter

All Rights Reserved

*Chatgpt: A Guide to Making Money With Chatgpt
(Creative Ways for Teens and Young Adults to
Make Money With Chatgpt)*

ISBN 978-1-7773611-8-1

All Rights Reserved

ISBN 978-1-7773611-8-1

No part of this guidebook shall be reproduced in any form without permission in writing from the publisher except in the case of brief quotations embodied in critical articles or reviews.

Legal & Disclaimer

The information contained in this book is not designed to replace or take the place of any form of medicine or professional medical advice. The information in this book has been provided for educational & entertainment purposes only.

The information contained in this book has been compiled from sources deemed reliable, and it is accurate to the best of the Author's knowledge; however, the Author cannot guarantee its accuracy and validity and cannot be held liable for any errors or omissions. Changes are periodically made to this book. You must consult your doctor or get professional medical advice before using any of the suggested remedies, techniques, or information in this book.

Table Of Contents

CHAPTER 1: What is Chat GPT?

ChatGPT modified into created thru the usage of OpenAI. Before we describe what it does. Let us speak some relevant terms. The AI in OpenAI stands for Artificial Intelligence. AI refers to laptop structures that carry out the shape of responsibilities usually requiring human intelligence. For instance Amazon's Alexa uses AI to recognize human speech and play the music, audiobooks or extraordinary audio content material that human beings may usually want to discover themselves. Google Maps makes use of AI to find out close by places the manner a human ought to generally have a look at a map and lots of others.

Chat GPT is a Large Language Model. Large language models (LLMs) are computer packages that technique the terms we supply them. They use Neural Networks. A

Neural community , is a method in Artificial Intelligence that teaches pc structures to device records much like the manner we suppose as human beings. It uses Natural Language Processing. This technique it strives to understand and reply to textual content or voice information then reply with text or speech much like the manner people do.

It has been professional on a big quantity of textual content located at the internet and has the ability to recognize and respond to herbal language. This makes it able to generating coherent, context-aware answers to numerous questions and prompts.

It makes use of deep studying strategies to analyze textual content and expect viable solutions based absolutely at the patterns it determined out in the course of its schooling. It then generates output this is regular with the tone, fashion, and content material material of the enter. This versatility makes it beneficial for some of applications, at the side of chatbots, content material fabric cloth creation, and facts assessment (to call however some).

One of the best advantages of ChatGPT is its ease of use and scalability. Unlike different language fashions that require specialized abilities or infrastructure, it could be protected into various systems and applications with minimal technical expertise. Plus, it is loose to get right of entry to and may be utilized by every person with a web connection.

In give up, ChatGPT is an advanced and bendy language version that has the potential to change how we engage with pc systems and method language. Its capability to generate responses which can be aware about context and its ease of use make it a sport-changer for a number of industries and programs.

History of ChatGPT

ChatGPT become superior via way of OpenAI, a research enterprise focused on synthetic intelligence. Version GPT 3.Five have become added in 2022, and is part of a circle of relatives of gadget getting to know models designed to and generate natural language. The GPT in ChatGPT stands for Generative Pre-professional Transformer. Probably because of the reality it's far based totally totally on a kind of tool getting to know called "transformer" models, which use big portions of facts and complex algorithms to research styles in language and generate human-like responses to text.

It is a part of a lineage of models evolved by using way of way of OpenAI, which incorporates the real GPT model brought in 2018, and next versions collectively with GPT-2 , GPT-3 and GPT-four. These models have received large interest for their capability to generate sensible and contextually-appropriate language in hundreds of settings, from chatbots to creative writing.

While it's data is pretty brief, its development is part of a larger style in the location of synthetic intelligence inside the path of extra brand new and human-like language processing fashions. As these fashions keep to conform and beautify, they've got the potential to revolutionize the way we communicate and interact with machines.

three How ChatGPT turn out to be informed

ChatGPT come to be expert the use of strategies known as unsupervised mastering and transformer-based language modeling. Without getting too technical, the ones include feeding huge quantities of textual content statistics into the model and allowing it to investigate patterns and relationships amongst phrases and terms on its personal, without any precise steering or supervision from human beings.

To train it, OpenAI used a large dataset of text from a various sort of property, consisting of online books, internet web sites, and one-of-a-kind on line content. This records come to be preprocessed and fed into the model in batches, with the version constantly adjusting itself to beautify its capacity to anticipate the subsequent word in a given sentence or piece of textual content.

The schooling system for ChatGPT changed into complex and time-consuming, regarding many rounds of experimentation and optimization to excellent-music the model's performance. OpenAI also used masses of techniques to beautify the variety and notable of the generated textual content, inclusive of incorporating a couple of education objectives and using a manner known as "temperature sampling" to govern the creativity of the generated responses.

Overall, the schooling method for it emerge as a outstanding feat of computational engineering and information processing, requiring huge belongings and recognise-the manner to attain the high levels of general performance that the version is able to.

four How to get commenced with ChatGPT and Chat GPT Prompts

In order to begin the use of ChatGPT, there are some things you can want to have. First, you will need a tool that may get proper of entry to the internet. This might be a pc laptop, laptop, or perhaps a cellular phone.

Next, you may need a web connection. It is to be had on-line, so that you'll need to be connected to the internet at the manner to apply it.

Finally, you will need a manner to engage with it. This may be accomplished through a web interface provided by means of the use of the usage of OpenAI, or via APIs (Application Programming Interfaces) furnished through way of OpenAI so that it will let you integrate it into your personal programs. An API is a difficult and rapid of protocols, physical games, and tool for building software and packages, and lets in conversation among top notch structures. In this education route we're able to specially be using an internet browser (which include Google Chrome or Firefox) to engage with it.

From there, you may start the use of it by way of moving into questions or prompts into the net interface and seeing the responses generated through the use of using the model.

If you need to use the APIs provided with the aid of OpenAI, you'll want to have a few technical understanding and a primary statistics of programming. The OpenAI internet web site gives

documentation and code samples that allow you to get commenced with the APIs, even if you are new to programming.

In short, getting commenced with it is easy and smooth, whether or not you're using the internet interface or the APIs. All you need is a web-related tool and a desire to find out the sector of conversational AI.

Starting ChatGPT on your Desktop Computer

To start using it for your computing tool pc, you'll need to follow these steps:

1. Visit the OpenAI internet web page at https://openai.Com/blog/chatgpt

2. If you do no longer have already got an account with OpenAI, click on the "Sign Up" button and create a modern account.

three. Once you have got were given signed in on your account, you could get right of access to the internet interface.

four. Enter a question or spark off into the textual content field supplied and click on on on the "Ask" button to appearance the response generated by way of it.

5. You're now prepared to start the use of ChatGPT!

Congratulations, you've got truely launched Chat GPT!

Quick ChatGPT check - using the net interface and our first activate

Now that you have a web-related device, permit's make certain it actually works. We will kind in our first spark off. A set off is the question or training we kind into chatgpt. We moreover communicate over with it as a question. Here's how to test the net interface with our first set off (which we can also talk to as a query):

1. Go to the OpenAI net website online and create an account when you have no longer already.

2. Log in to your account and navigate to the it phase.

three. You need to see a text box in which you may enter a hard and fast off or query.

four. Try entering a simple set off, such as "What is the which means of existence?"

five. Hit the "Submit" button to look it's far response.

6.   You need to see it is generated reaction displayed under the textual content container.

To kingdom the apparent, ChatGPT need for use to assist make life easier for us, however can not inform us the this means that of lifestyles or what we have to do not forget. Therefore I need to emphasise that we need to continually do our non-public research, no matter what it may inform us. Rather than the bearer of truth, I suggest we use it as a beneficial productiveness tool. With that in thoughts, congratulations! You have truely effectively tested ChatGPT the usage of the internet interface.

CHAPTER 2: How to Use ChatGPT to Start and Grow Any Business

Whether you're running for someone else's industrial enterprise enterprise or growing your own, enterprise business enterprise can be tough, particularly even as you're confronted with obstacles which you do no longer understand how to conquer or want to triumph over speedy. This is in which ChatGPT can assist. It is an AI-powered tool that permit you to increase your organisation by providing insights, answers and automation to issues that you could no longer even apprehend exist.

One of the strategies in which it let you boom your organisation is via identifying regions in which you may be able to decorate. It can not most effective provide you with ideas, however furthermore examine enterprise employer data. This consists of income, advertising and advertising and marketing, and client statistics, to discover areas in which you will be falling quick or lacking possibilities. By identifying these regions, it will can help you to obtain this and make improvements to develop your corporation.

Another way wherein it assist you to make bigger your business agency is by using using manner of providing insights into your customers. It can examine purchaser statistics, at the side in their behaviors and options, that will help you apprehend your customers higher. This allow you to to tailor your services and products to meet their desires, ensuing in more satisfied customers and multiplied earnings.

It also can assist you to create content and optimize your advertising efforts. By reading your target sell it will let you to create applicable textual content, snap shots and distinct media so that you have incredible, centered advertising campaigns which can be more likely to acquire achievement. This will let you to get more completed in a fragment of the time, make your manage crew satisfied in case you work for a person else, and attraction to extra customers on your very own enterprise organisation.

One of the most interesting subjects is that whether or not you figure for your self or someone else, it will let you make extra cash. I is probably showing you methods in this schooling so stay tuned for the right techniques you may use these days!

In summary, ChatGPT can be a beneficial tool for being extremely good-powerful and developing a business commercial enterprise company whilst you do now not know what you do now not recognise. By analyzing statistics, developing content material material, identifying regions for improvement, and providing insights into your customers and marketing efforts, it will can help you to blow up your productivity and make extra cash for any enterprise business enterprise. Whether you are an worker, startup, walking solo or an established industrial organization, ChatGPT will allow you to to advantage your dreams quicker than ever earlier than!

What is the Best Business to Start with ChatGPT

Whether you're strolling for a company employer and need to earn extra cash or an entrepreneur growing your commercial agency. You want to preserve in thoughts incorporating ChatGPT into your plans. In this chapter, we're in a function to speak some of the quality makes use of and companies to start with it.

1. Content Creation

One of the most famous uses of ChatGPT is the generation of content material material, textual content and pictures that may be utilized in social media, ebooks or anywhere your company goals. This can assist businesses to turn out to be a long way greater efficient. Even if a Social Media Marketing professional or assistant though consists of out the duties, it is able to help them to be a protracted way more powerful in a shorter region of time.

2. Social Media Marketing

It may be used to analyze social media facts and provide insights on customer behavior, hobbies, and alternatives. This information can be used to tailor social media campaigns and beautify engagement. It additionally may be used to generate social media ad replica and headlines which can be optimized for maximum click on on-via prices and conversions. The content material cloth from the content material creation duties additionally can be covered into social media posts and associated blogs.

3. Customer Service Automation

One of the maximum sincere programs of it's miles in customer support automation. Companies can use it to create chatbots that provide 24/7 customer support, solution often asked questions, and deal with easy client inquiries. This can store agencies time and belongings, in addition to beautify the consumer revel in via presenting set off and personalized guide. Emails may be generated that answer clients' maximum commonplace queries.

4. Virtual Personal Assistants

Another capability agency opportunity with it's far within the advent of digital private assistants. It may be used to create AI-powered non-public assistants that help individuals manipulate their schedules, make pointers, and answer questions. This form of generation has the capability to be fantastically beneficial for busy human beings and may be protected into a number of awesome services and products.

5. Language Translation

Finally, it can be used to increase AI-powered language translation offerings. It has been knowledgeable on a huge corpus of text in multiple languages, making it properly-appropriate for translation obligations. Businesses that specialize in language translation offerings can use it to provide quicker and extra accurate translations, which can be specially beneficial for organizations jogging in more than one international places or serving a global purchaser base.

In give up, ChatGPT has the capacity to revolutionize many one-of-a-kind industries and offer you with numerous commercial enterprise opportunities. Whether you're searching for to automate customer support, create more appealing advertising and advertising and marketing reports, or growth digital private assistants, it permit you to acquire your desires and develop your commercial enterprise business enterprise.

These mind are truely the quit of the iceberg. I may be displaying you the manner you can use the ones and additional mind to extend your horizons and make extra money in your organization.

How to Generate Emails with ChatGPT

ChatGPT can be a tremendous tool to help you write powerful emails fast. Whether you're sending a brief notice to a colleague or a longer email to a consumer, it assist you to discover the proper phrases and phrasing to get your message across efficiently.

With its advanced language era competencies, it can save you time and enhance your electronic mail writing competencies.

Let's get commenced with our first sales e-mail:

Type in query: "write a sales electronic mail to promote tshirts to customers of our tshirt emblem"

Using it for e-mail writing has numerous blessings. It will let you keep time as you might not have to spend hours looking to give you the right phrases or phraseology.

Additionally, it will let you improve your e-mail writing talents by using supplying you with a start line and presenting guidelines for words and phrasing that you won't have notion of in your personal.

Type in query: "improve the sales e mail to encompass key phrases that get the consumer's interest"

We can also write a 3 component email, usually utilized by entrepreneurs to promote merchandise.

Type in query: "write a three component sales email. Each electronic mail to be sent on a one-of-a-kind day and each electronic mail with a subject line that gets customers to open the e-mail to buy a tshirt"

With its ease of use, every person can begin using it for e mail writing in only some mins. All you need is access to the OpenAI internet site and a login to their platform. So whether you are a busy entrepreneur, a marketing professional, or just a person who wants to write better emails, it's far the appropriate tool that will help you get the job carried out.

In conclusion, if you're looking for a way to jot down higher emails in much less time, it's miles the suitable device for you. With its advanced language generation competencies, ease of use, and potential to prevent time, it's miles the precise answer for every person seeking to enhance their e mail writing skills.

CHAPTER 3: How to Use ChatGPT as a Search Engine

Although ChatGPT has the ability to reply questions, generate textual content, and perform lots of other obligations. One capacity use for it's miles as a seek engine.

To use it as a seek engine, all you want to do is input a question or query into the interface, and the model will generate a reaction. This reaction can include statistics on a variety of subjects, which include contemporary events, historic events, and greater.

For example. Let's suppose we want to analyze thoughts for our new enterprise. We're interested by promoting t shirts on-line. We've determined to use it to guide us on this journey.

Type in the query: "what's the pleasant manner to begin a print on demand t-shirt enterprise"

As you can see, it has not given you a listing of pages from across the net (like Google does). It has summarized a number of steps based totally on it's education. Almost like an guide or assistant guide. Of path we have to bear in thoughts that the outcomes should be established. However that is a very beneficial place to begin and time saver.

One gain of the usage of it as a seek engine is that it presents a greater conversational, interactive revel in. Instead of surely typing in a query and receiving a listing of results, you could engage in a returned-and-forth communication with it to get the data you need. This may be specially beneficial when you have a complicated or multi-component question that requires greater than a easy search query.

Let's studies one among it's endorsed print on-demand platforms to print T-Shirts for our new enterprise.

Type in question: "how to setup a tshirt logo on teespring in underneath 10 steps"

Another gain of it's far that it is able to provide records that is not without difficulty located through conventional search engines like google and yahoo like Google. This is because it's far skilled on a huge form of text from the internet, along with articles, boards, and more. This lets in it to offer more comprehensive and diverse solutions to questions.

That being said, it is essential to word that it isn't always designed to update Google or other traditional engines like google. It is better suitable for answering specific questions, generating text, and acting different AI-related obligations, whereas Google is designed to offer a comprehensive index of the web and to assist customers find applicable records via search queries.

In end, whilst ChatGPT can be used as a seek engine, it's no longer intended to update traditional search engines like google and yahoo like Google. Instead, it offers a unique and interactive revel in for customers who want to invite questions and acquire solutions in a conversational way.

Doing SEO Basics with ChatGPT

Search Engine Optimization or SEO is a method that facilitates to optimize a website for search engines. The fundamental aim of search engine marketing is to enhance the visibility and rating of a internet site in seek engine end result pages (SERP). It is an essential device that may help it to draw more users and enhance its online presence.

The first step in search engine optimization is key-word research. Keywords are the phrases or phrases that customers type inside the seek engine to find relevant data. It can use numerous tools like Google Keyword Planner, Ahrefs, and SEMrush to perceive the relevant key phrases for the internet site.

Type in question: "discover the pinnacle 10 key phrases to apply on our ecommerce website to promote t shirts"

Of route for a real commercial enterprise, you could want to kind in a more precise query and verify the key phrases are suitable, but you get the point.

Once the key phrases are identified, the following step is to optimize the on-page elements. On-web page optimization includes optimizing page titles, meta descriptions, header tags, and content. By including the applicable key phrases in the content, it is able to make the website greater readable and engaging for the users.

Type in query: "optimize the following name the use of one or extra of the keywords we discovered "Grab Your T-Shirt Today""

The technical elements of the internet site can also be optimized to make it simpler for seek engine bots to move slowly and index the pages. It can optimize internet site pace, cellular-friendliness, and website shape to enhance the website's ranking.

Type in question: "Which coding or improvement strategies may be used to optimize a website's velocity, and the way can they be implemented"

Link constructing is some other essential thing of search engine optimization. By constructing exquisite one way links and on web site links, ChatGPT can improve the website's authority and popularity within the eyes of search engines. Guest posting, blogger outreach, and developing terrific content are some of the approaches to construct hyperlinks. These are outside the scope of this training, but you can use it to indicate the pleasant vicinity to seize hyperlinks from or the way to create links on the way to growth your rating on the search engines like google and yahoo.

Local search engine marketing is every other critical element of search engine marketing. This allows your commercial enterprise display up to humans searching for businesses of their nearby place. If your store has a bodily presence, then it's far essential to optimize the website for nearby seek. Creating neighborhood listings, creating the Google My Business web page, and including place-particular key phrases within the content material can enhance the website's visibility.

Type in question: "generate the content material for the google my enterprise page listing for a tshirt"

When we run our query, it now not best generates a description but has even created a dummy cope with. This facilitates us to visualise the completed My Business Listing extra without problems. We can constantly change, lessen or increase the textual content to our delight.

In conclusion, search engine marketing is a non-stop system, and ChatGPT can help us constantly rise to the pinnacle of search listings. By implementing the above search engine marketing basics, it may improve its search engine scores, appeal to more customers, and growth revenue for any commercial enterprise.

CHAPTER 4: How to Write Blogs with ChatGPT

ChatGPT can be a beneficial device for blog writing. By leveraging its herbal language processing abilties, it is able to generate outstanding content material this is enticing, informative, and tailored to the wishes of the target market. This may be especially useful for individuals or organizations that need to produce a huge volume of content on a regular foundation.

One of the blessings of the usage of it for weblog writing is that it may save time and effort. Instead of spending hours learning, writing or buying content material, it is able to generate a draft that includes key factors and ideas for the weblog submit. This may be especially useful for busy bloggers or content entrepreneurs who need to supply a high volume of content material on a ordinary basis.

Type in question: "Create a 2 hundred word weblog put up known as "Why T shirts are taking America By Storm""

We now have a small weblog submit we will reality-discover, re-write and then use for our purposes.

Another advantage of the use of it for weblog writing is that it is able to assist make sure the content is nicely-organized and based. It can analyze the textual content and offer tips for the introduction, essential frame, and conclusion of the weblog publish. This can assist to make certain that the content material flows logically and is easy for the reader to comply with.

Type in question: "Update the above blog post so it has an creation, important frame and conclusion."

We can in addition decorate the post with titles key-word optimized for S.E.O as follows:

Type in question: "update the above blog publish so it has keyword optimized titles for the introduction, foremost frame and end which are relevant for a t blouse ecommerce internet site"

However, as always it's far vital to be aware that even as it is able to generate incredible content material, it isn't an alternative choice to a human author. Human writers can offer a completely unique perspective and writing fashion that ChatGPT might not be able to reflect. Also, we have referred to in some instances that content material may additionally contain inaccuracies. Therefore, it's far advocated to have a human author evaluation and edit the content generated via it to ensure its exceptional and accuracy.

In summary, ChatGPT can be a useful tool for blog writing, specially for individuals or businesses that want to provide a excessive quantity of content on a normal basis. While it could shop effort and time and provide recommendations for organizing the content, it isn't an alternative choice to a human writer and need to be used in conjunction with human modifying and assessment.

How to Do Social Media Marketing with ChatGPT

Social media has grow to be an imperative part of modern-day advertising and marketing, and organizations of all sizes are the use of social media to connect to their audiences and promote their products and services. However, developing and executing a social media marketing strategy can be time-eating and difficult, especially for small companies with constrained sources. One solution that groups can explore is the usage of ChatGPT for social media advertising and marketing.

It is an AI-based totally device that uses herbal language processing to generate tremendous content material, including social media posts, captions, and hashtags. By the use of it for social media advertising, businesses can shop time and resources while nonetheless developing remarkable content material that resonates with their audience.

Here are some approaches wherein organizations can use it for social media advertising and marketing:

1. Content introduction: It can generate ideas and create content material for social media posts and captions. It can offer tips for content subjects, headlines, and duplicate, making it less difficult for

agencies to create notable content material quickly.

2. Hashtag era: It can analyze the content material of social media posts and advise relevant hashtags that can help boom the visibility of the submit.

3. Content optimization: It can examine the content material of social media posts and advocate adjustments to improve the quality and effectiveness of the content material. This can encompass suggestions on the duration of the post, the usage of pics and films, and the overall tone of the content.

4. Personalization: It may be educated to apprehend the target market of a commercial enterprise and generate content material that resonates with that target market. This can help companies create extra personalized and engaging

content material that drives greater engagement and conversions.

five. A/B checking out: It can generate a couple of versions of social media posts and captions, permitting groups to test which version performs better. This can help organizations optimize their social media content material and improve their ordinary social media advertising method.

Type in question: "Generate hashtags for the Instagram account for our ecommerce tshirt enterprise."

See the way it now not most effective gives us key phrases, however additional pointers about along with region-applicable hashtags.

While it could be a powerful device for social media advertising, it is crucial to be aware that it isn't a substitute for a human social media marketer.

In end, ChatGPT may be a precious tool for agencies seeking to improve their social media advertising approach. By using it to generate content material and optimize their social media presence, businesses can keep time and sources whilst nevertheless developing high-quality content material that resonates with their target audience.

CHAPTER 5: How to Create Social Media Posts with ChatGPT

Social media has come to be an vital a part of our each day lives, and it has revolutionized the manner we communicate and have interaction with others. With billions of customers international, social media systems have grow to be a powerful device for corporations to reach their target market and promote their logo.

Creating attractive social media posts is critical to capture the eye of your audience, and that's in which ChatGPT can assist. As a huge language version trained through OpenAI, it is able to offer you with treasured insights and tips to create powerful social media posts that resonate together with your target market.

In this lesson, we will explore the exceptional methods in which ChatGPT can help you create social media posts that get observed and drive engagement.

1.   Understanding your target market: It can analyze your audience's conduct, pastimes, and preferences to help you tailor your social media posts to their liking. By know-how what your target audience desires, you can create posts that are more likely to get engagement and shares.

Type in question: "discover what are the pinnacle 5 most popular styles of tshirts and what form of humans are buying them"

Here, it's far cautious to say that it does no longer have the trendy income facts, however can give you a large wide variety of popular developments to factor you within the right route on your daily work or commercial enterprise.

Type in query: "offer a 50 phrase fb put up on how I may explain to someone why they may like the featured t-blouse"

2.   Generating ideas for social media posts: If you are stuck in a rut and don't know what to post, it is able to provide you with creative ideas and pointers for your social media posts. Whether you need ideas for Instagram, Facebook, Twitter, or LinkedIn, it let you brainstorm new and interesting content ideas.

Type in question: "create a quick instagram version of the above publish with characters and emojis people on instagram will like"

3.   Crafting compelling headlines and captions: Headlines and captions are the first things that humans see after they come across your social media posts. ChatGPT will let you craft catchy headlines and captions that capture your target

audience's interest and encourage them to engage along with your post.

Type in query: "create a caption for the above put up that could entice interest on instagram"

Notice how this time the caption is extra relevant and captures your attention extra.

four. Writing social media posts that convert: Creating social media posts that convert your target market into clients is critical for business success. ChatGPT assist you to create persuasive posts that encourage your audience to do so, which includes making a purchase, signing up for a publication, or sharing your content.

By the usage of it to create your social media posts, you can shop time, boost engagement, and force greater visitors for your website. Whether you're a commercial enterprise owner, marketer, or social media manager, it will let you create powerful social media posts that get excellent results.

How to Write Linkedin Profiles and Articles with ChatGPT

ChatGPT can be an effective tool for writing LinkedIn profiles and articles. By using its natural language processing abilities, it is able to speedy generate extremely good content material that is tailor-made to the expert wishes of the target market. This may be specially beneficial for busy specialists who need to create a strong LinkedIn profile and regularly submit articles.

One of the advantages of using it for LinkedIn profile and article writing is that it could keep time and effort. Instead of spending hours studying and writing content material, it may generate a draft that consists of key data and ideas for the profile or article. This may be in particular beneficial for busy professionals who have restrained time to commit to their LinkedIn profile and publishing articles.

Type in question: "Generate a linkedin profile for the CEO of a tshirt ecommerce brand."

Look at the element inside every segment. You might have idea it was written by a actual character, proper? While we do no longer need any untruths on our profiles, this will function a top notch start line or inspiration on your profile. It can then be tweaked and up to date with correct, actual existence information.

Another advantage of the usage of it for LinkedIn profile and article writing is that it could help ensure the content is properly-organized and established. It can examine the text and offer pointers to ensure that the content material flows logically and is easy for the reader to follow.

Type in query: "Generate a linkedin post for the tshirt ecommerce logo."

In precis, ChatGPT can be a powerful device for writing LinkedIn profiles and articles, particularly for busy professionals who want to create a fantastic profile quickly. While it could shop effort and time and provide recommendations for organizing the profile and posts, it isn't an alternative choice to the human touch and should be used along side human editing and evaluation.

How to Use Copy.Ai for Instagram Captions

Instagram has end up a famous platform for companies and individuals to promote their logo, merchandise, and offerings. One of the most essential factors of Instagram advertising and marketing is developing engaging captions that seize the attention of your target audience and encourage them to interact with your content material.

Although ChatGPT can be used to generate decent Instagram captions, some people like to apply other AI tools to have additional manage over their captions and content material.

Copy.Ai is an AI-powered writing tool that can help you create captivating Instagram captions in seconds. With its advanced language processing competencies, it permit you to generate unique and creative captions that resonate together with your target audience.

First, permit's use ChatGPT to inform us how we can create an account on Copy.Ai

Type in query: "a way to create a loose account for reproduction ai"

The copy.Ai home page and sign on page must seem like the beneath. Note that the join up commands observed on ChatGPT can be barely specific since it changed into trained on statistics from an in advance term. Luckily we are able to exercise session how to sign on for ourselves.

Once in the reproduction.Ai app, it's time to create a few captions.

We will discover the one-of-a-kind approaches in which you may use it to create compelling Instagram captions that get observed and power engagement:

1. Understanding your target audience: Before you start, it's crucial to recognize your target audience. This includes their pastimes, pain points, and alternatives. With this understanding, you can create captions which are tailor-made to their want and desires. We did this formerly.

2. Generating ideas: It allow you to generate thoughts to your Instagram captions quickly. All you want to do is offer the device with a few key phrases related to your content or topic, and it's going to generate multiple caption options that you can use or regulate to suit your brand voice.

Type in query: "create ideas for instagram captions for our tshirt posts the usage of a number of those keywords: Trendy T-Shirts, High - Quality Fabric, Comfortable T-Shirts, Unique Designs, Affordable Prices, Stylish T-shirts, Customizable T-Shirts, Fashionable T-Shirts, Soft T-Shirts, Durable T-Shirts"

As you may see, 10 caption ideas have been created right away.

three. Crafting the perfect caption: Once you have generated a few ideas, you can use it to refine your captions in addition.

The device permit you to adjust the tone, fashion, and length of your caption to healthy your brand voice and appeal for your audience. You can use the drop down menus on the page to try this.

You will then see more than one versions of your text with improvements ordinary with the alternatives you chose. Feel loose to select out whichever works great.

4.   Testing and refining: Like any marketing method, it is crucial to test your Instagram captions to look how your audience responds to them. Copy.Ai allow you to analyze the general normal performance of your captions and offer you with insights at the manner to beautify them in addition. We have typed in a query to do this, however you can moreover use a number of the tool's special talents to further enhance your advertisements, captions and content material cloth.

Type in query: "study the overall universal overall performance of the captions above and offer insights on a manner to enhance them"

By using Copy.Ai for your Instagram captions, you may shop time, boom engagement, and create extra impactful content cloth that resonates along with your target audience. Whether you are a organization proprietor, worker, marketer, or social media manager, this could assist you create charming Instagram captions that get outcomes.

CHAPTER 6: How to Use ChatGPT for Language Translation

ChatGPT is an AI-powered device that assist you to overcome language obstacles through providing accurate and inexperienced translation offerings. With its herbal language processing abilties, It can translate textual content from one language to a few different brief and as it should be.

To use it for language translation, you truely need to go into the text you need to translate and decide the source and aim languages. It will then study the text, thinking of the context, idiomatic expressions, and cultural references to offer an accurate and enormous translation.

Type in question: "translate "Looking for a t-blouse that's every snug and fashionable? Look no further! Our featured t-blouse is made from immoderate – pleasant substances which might be gentle at the pores and pores and skin and lengthy – lasting. Plus, it's present day day layout is sure to show heads wherever you bypass. Don't skip over out on this need to – have addition to your cloth cabinet!" into French, taking into account Parisian way of life and expressions"

To evaluate permit's visit Google Translate and kind within the identical paragraph. We can use ChatGPT to tell us the way to translate the facebook positioned up in google translate.

Type in question: "a manner to translate a facebook put up in google translate"

Now if we run the steps in Google Translate with our fb located up we get the following.

As you may see the output is a touch particular in the Google translate version.

Probably because of the reality we counseled it to recollect Parisian tradition and expressions

One of the benefits of using ChatGPT for language translation is that it can translate more than one languages, making it less complicated to talk with those who communicate one-of-a-kind languages. You can input text in a unmarried language and get an correct translation in some unique language in seconds.

It additionally allows you to customize your translations to suit your unique needs. For instance, you can select to translate a proper or casual tone or pick company-precise phrases and jargon. This can help ensure that your translations are accurate and applicable in your target marketplace.

Type in question: "translate our remaining Facebook put up into French in a extra formal tone than earlier than, however deliberating Parisian lifestyle"

Note the variations inside the translation now that we've informed ChaGPT to translate our last Facebook post into French in a extra formal tone than before.

Unlike exceptional translation offerings, as you continue to use ChatGPT for language translation, the tool will study and beautify over time. This method that translations turns into extra correct and customized to your precise goals. Additionally, it could offer you with remarks to your translations, permitting you to find out regions for improvement and refine your translation competencies.

We of course advocate you to get the interpretation checked over through a person who's conscious the language you're translating to.

In precis, using ChatGPT for language translation permit you to keep time and enhance conversation with folks that communicate remarkable languages. Whether you're a business enterprise owner, traveler, or language learner, it permit you to talk greater efficaciously and correctly.

How to apply ChatGPT to Write Youtube Scripts

ChatGPT can be used to generate Youtube video scripts rapid and with out issue.

Type in query: "generate a script for a promo for our new t-shirt (one of the tshirt patterns described earlier)"

As you may see, it has generated a script that directs what is visible inside the video, further to showing the phrases that need to be spoken. This may be used to generate beneficial scripts which may be coherent and applicable on your topic.

One of the blessings of the usage of it for Youtube scripts is that it may prevent some of time. Instead of typing out your script, you could use it to generate it fast and efficiently then edit it as you spot wholesome. This will can help you to create greater content material in a whole lot much less time and be greater effective.

Additionally, this may assist you to enhance the fantastic of your Youtube scripts. By the use of it to generate the script, you can cognizance greater on the content material and transport of the message, resulting in a extra herbal and attractive video. This can assist to increase your viewership and engagement on your Youtube channel.

Type in query: "generate the identical script with more of an exciting transport"

Notice the way it has brought turns on to feature satisfaction inside the video similarly to delight in the narration.

In precis, the usage of ChatGPT will will let you to generate brilliant Youtube scripts short and successfully. By doing this, you can keep time and beautify the high-quality of your content material fabric fabric, resulting in extra engaging and effective motion pix.

CHAPTER 7: How to Use ChatGPT to Create Podcast Scripts

In contemporary years, podcasts have obtained high-quality recognition, with increasingly more human beings tuning in to take note of their favorite shows. If you are thinking of beginning a podcast, one of the most critical belongings you need is a extraordinary script. A nicely-written script will allow you to stay heading inside the right path, preserve your target audience engaged, and supply your message successfully. However, growing a podcast script from scratch may be time-eating and hard. That's in which ChatGPT is available in - it's far an AI-powered device that assist you to assemble a podcast script in just mins. Here's how:

Step 1: Identify the Purpose and Topic of Your Podcast

Before you begin writing your podcast script, you need to have a clear concept of what you want to gather together together with your podcast and what subject matter you need to cover. You can use it to generate mind for podcast topics based totally mostly on your interests, enterprise, or area of interest. Once you have got a topic in thoughts, you may flow into immediately to the subsequent step.

Step 2: Use ChatGPT to Generate a Basic Outline

Now that you have a topic in thoughts, you may use it to generate a simple outline for your podcast script. It allow you to find out the important thing factors you want to cover in your podcast and get them organized in a logical order. Simply input your difficulty rely into it, and it's going to generate a fundamental define for you in handiest minutes.

Type in question: "create a primary define for a hundred word podcast script for a podcast known as: The trade entrepreneur podcast."

ChatGPT has created a podcast outline with timings and thoughts for communicate points.

Step three: Customize and Edit Your Script

Once you've got got a number one define, you may customise it to suit your style, tone, and choices. You can use it to generate precise thoughts, phrases, and sentences in your podcast script. It additionally allow you to adjust the period and form of your script to in shape the time constraints of your podcast.

Type in query: "adjust the duration and form of the script to healthful internal of 15 seconds"

The outline now fits within 15 seconds. This can be used as an Intro.

Step four: Refine Your Script with ChatGPT

After you have got were given have been given customized your script, you can use it to refine it in addition. It can help you add depth, nuance, and persona for your script thru suggesting specific terms, terms, and idioms that in shape your subject matter and tone. You also can use it to make sure that your script is grammatically correct and blunders-free.

Type in question: "recommend unique words, terms, and idioms that wholesome the above venture be counted and tone"

We now have a number of pointers for words and phrases that healthful the problem and tone of the podcast.

Step five: Practice and Record Your Podcast

Once you've got got finalized your podcast script, you can workout and record your podcast. With ChatGPT, you could have a professional-great script in simplest mins, presenting you with extra time to popularity on delivering an interesting and informative podcast.

In quit, building a podcast script can be a time-ingesting and hard gadget, but with ChatGPT, you could create a professional-notable script in best minutes. By following those easy steps, you could leverage the strength of AI to create a podcast script that engages your target audience and promises your message successfully. You can increase upon a simple outline until you've got were given enough content for hours of discussion!

How to Write Reports with ChatGPT

Report writing is an essential part of many professions, which encompass commercial business employer, academia, and studies. It calls for the capability to investigate and installation records, and to provide that facts in a smooth and concise manner.

ChatGPT may be a beneficial tool for document writing, as it may help clients to generate insights and mind, shape their record, and beautify their writing style.

One of the benefits of the use of it for document writing is that it will let you to generate insights and thoughts that you could no longer have taken into consideration in advance than. By inputting your problem be counted or studies query, it can study relevant facts and provide guidelines for capability conclusions or insights. This let you to come to be aware of regions that you could have neglected or unnoticed, and might bring about a more complete and nicely-knowledgeable report.

Type in question: "Create 10 record thoughts approximately t shirts that might be beneficial for tshirt customers"

This has given us a list of report mind we will use as creatives. We can usually change them or talk with a set to enhance them. However they'll be a outstanding starting point.

Another benefit of the use of it for record writing is that it permit you to to shape your file. It can offer recommendations for the enterprise and waft of your record, similarly to suggestions for headings and subheadings. This will will permit you to to create a record that is nicely-organized and easy to navigate, that may make it greater to be had and appealing in your target marketplace.

Type in query: "Generate a 500 word document the usage of one of the above subjects"

It is smart sufficient to pick out out one of the subjects it gave us and write a whole record about it.

Now allow's offer it some extra form.

Type in question: "Create the proper heading and severa subheadings to provide the file form, if it does no longer have already got one"

Once we've have been given the structure looked after, we're able to even make the record extra readable for the target audience.

Type in question: "enhance the drift of the record to make it as readable as viable for the reader"

Now that clarity has been taken care of we're able to take a look at the writing fashion. It assist you to to beautify your writing fashion via way of using reading your writing and offering guidelines for grammar, sentence shape, and word desire. This permit you to to create a document this is greater polished and professional.

Type in query: "Suggest upgrades for the writing fashion, grammar, sentence form, and word preference inside the following document: "

These changes can help to enhance the credibility and authority of your report, and may make it more compelling for your target audience.

In precis, ChatGPT can be a beneficial tool for record writing, because it can help you to generate insights and ideas, shape your record, and enhance your writing style. Whether you are writing a employer document, research paper, or academic essay, it can help you to create a document that is nicely-knowledgeable, well-organized, and well-written.

How to Script and Write Presentations with ChatGPT

Presentation scripting and writing is a vital detail of public speaking and handing over effective suggests. Chat GPT can be an remarkable tool that will help you put together a presentation script this is attractive, informative and tailor-made on your target market.

One of the benefits of using it for presentation scripting and writing is that it's going to will let you to generate thoughts and insights that you may no longer have taken into consideration earlier than. By inputting your presentation problem rely or studies question, it is able to study relevant information and offer hints for ability conclusions, insights, or perhaps provide you with relevant stories that might resonate together with your target audience. This will let you to understand new regions of records that you may have disregarded, and might result in a greater comprehensive and properly-informed presentation.

Type in question: "Create a two hundred phrase presentation on a manner to create a tshirt corporation."

Another advantage of the use of it for presentation scripting and writing is that it let you to form your presentation. It can offer hints for the organization and go with the float of your presentation, further to guidelines for headings and subheadings. This can help you to create a presentation that is nicely-organized and smooth to have a look at, that could make it greater on hand and engaging to your target market.

Type in query: "Suggest upgrades to the organisation and waft of the above presentation, consisting of headings and subheadings"

This is obviously the skeleton of the presentation. It can be greater suitable and fleshed out in more detail through way of focussing on each factor.

Furthermore, it can help you to decorate your writing fashion, and the language you use in your presentation. By reading your writing and imparting suggestions for grammar, sentence shape, and phrase choice, it'll permit you to to create a presentation script that is greater polished and expert. This can assist to beautify the credibility and authority of your presentation and can make it extra persuasive on your audience.

Type in question: "Suggest upgrades to the writing fashion of the above presentation collectively with grammar, sentence shape and word preference."

As you could see, ChatGPT will offer you with every pointers and precise examples of the manner to use those guidelines in your presentation. It is aware about special varieties of voice, sentence form, and the way you may combine the ones patterns to acquire your presentation reason. Again, you may move deeper into any a part of the presentation to get extra tips to attain great consequences along aspect your presentation.

In summary, Chat GPT can be an high-quality tool for presentation scripting and writing, because it will let you to generate new thoughts, shape your presentation efficiently, and decorate your writing style. Whether you are delivering a presentation to a industrial enterprise audience, a conference, or a fixed of college college students, it's going to will let you to create a presentation this is nicely-informed, properly-prepared, and nicely-written.

CHAPTER 8: How to Summarize Large Documents with ChatGPT

ChatGPT may be an powerful tool for fast summarizing big or maybe huge documents, such as critiques, research papers, and articles. By studying the text and extracting the most essential statistics, it may generate a concise and correct precis that highlights the vital issue factors of the file.

One of the benefits of using it for summarizing lengthy files is that it could hold time and enhance normal performance. Instead of studying through a prolonged file in its entirety, it could offer a precis that captures the most crucial records in simplest a fragment of the time. This may be mainly useful for professionals who need to check a big quantity of documents on a ordinary foundation.

Agile Scrum is a framework used for handing over tasks. Suppose we had been considering using it to run initiatives in our T Shirt enterprise. Let's perform a touch studies. We will start thru statistics and summarizing the rule of thumb of thumb-ebook of Agile Scrum, referred to as The Scrum Guide.

Type in query: "summarize the Scrum Guide in order that I can deliver an reason for how Agile Scrum may be utilized to deliver projects"

ChatGPT creates a precis. Please be conscious that there may be inaccuracies inside the output. For example, as a Scrum Master myself, I apprehend that the contemporary-day Scrum Guide now refers to the Development group as Developers, whilst you bear in mind that they need to now not be notion of as a separate organization. Due to such inaccuracies we generally suggest you use

ChatGPT as a tool to simplify your artwork and get it checked thru someone who can confirm the facts.

Additionally, this summary can be custom designed to reflect considered one of a kind patterns and codecs for summarizing documents. For example, it may be set to offer a short compare, an intensive summary, or a bullet-point list of the critical element factors. This flexibility could make ChatGPT a bendy device that may be carried out in severa contexts, along facet commercial enterprise enterprise, academia, and research.

Type in query: "Re-generate the above precis as a bullet-factor listing of key factors."

In summary, ChatGPT may be an green and powerful tool for summarizing prolonged files, as it could keep time, beautify the wonderful of the precis, and be custom designed to in shape high-quality styles and codecs. By the use of it to rapid summarize prolonged documents, specialists can boom their productivity and awareness at the maximum critical records.

How to Develop Technical Skills with ChatGPT

Hard capabilities are technical capabilities which may be unique to a particular place or organization, which includes coding, statistics evaluation, or engineering. ChatGPT can be an effective tool for hard expertise education and hassle-solving, as it could assist people to enhance their technical talents and provide insights and suggestions for solving complex problems.

One of the advantages of using it for hard capability schooling is that it could provide individuals with personalised hints for enhancing their technical talents. By reading an character's contemporary capacity diploma and dreams, it may recommend unique studying sources, together with tutorials, courses, and on-line property, which is probably tailor-made to the individual's desires. This can help people to attention their efforts on regions a awesome way to have the maximum effect on their not unusual hard abilties.

Another advantage of using it for hassle-fixing is that it can provide insights and suggestions for solving complicated troubles. By inputting records approximately the trouble, together with relevant information and constraints, it is able to take a look at the hassle and offer tips for capability solutions. This can help people to find out new strategies and techniques for solving problems that they may no longer have considered in advance than.

Type in query: "what shape of systems, software application software and equipment should I want to construct an iphone app for our internet website."

Type in query: "what sort of competencies might my institution need to construct the above app."

Furthermore, it is able to offer ongoing help and steerage for individuals who are going for walks to enhance their difficult abilties and hassle-fixing competencies. Through regular test-ins and personalised schooling, it can assist people to stay on course with their studying and make non-prevent progress closer to their desires.

Type in question: "Show me 5 education publications my group can take to get the above skills and wherein can we discover them on-line."

In precis, ChatGPT may be a treasured tool for hard expertise education and hassle-fixing, as it may provide personalized guidelines for reading and insights for fixing complicated problems. By enhancing their tough talents and problem-fixing capabilities, humans can decorate their usual performance and achievement of their field, that may lead to a more thrilling and profitable profession.

How to Write Sales Copy for Webpages with ChatGPT

ChatGPT may be a powerful tool for income copywriting on webpages.

Type in query: "what is income copywriting"

As noted in the output, sales copywriting makes use of the electricity of phrases to hold a message to a potential consumer with a purpose to sell them a services or products. This message in written form is called "replica".

By leveraging its natural language processing talents, ChatGPT can short generate top notch duplicate this is tailor-made to the goals of the target market and designed to convert site traffic into customers. This can be mainly beneficial for companies or those who need to create compelling and persuasive duplicate for their net internet sites.

One of the benefits of the use of it for copywriting webpages is that it could shop effort and time. Instead of spending hours mastering and writing copy, it may quick generate a draft that consists of key selling elements and persuasive language. This can be particularly beneficial for busy industrial employer proprietors or marketers who need to create replica for more than one webpages.

Another gain of the usage of it for copywriting webpages is that it is able to help ensure the reproduction relies and organized in a way that is simple for the reader to examine. ChatGPT can examine the textual content and provide pointers for the headline, subheadings, and frame textual content of the internet internet site. This can help to make certain that the duplicate is obvious, concise, and clean for the reader to recognize.

Type in query: "Create hundred phrases of compelling income reproduction for a brand new reversable tshirt."

Now permit's beautify our sales reproduction by way of way of optimizing it for the serps like google and yahoo.

Type in question: "Update the above to encompass suitable key-word optimized headlines and subheadings."

Now let's go even similarly to focus on key promoting factors for our clients.

Type in question: "Update the above to embody a separate phase with bullet pointed key selling points along aspect a key-phrase optimized phase heading."

As commonplace, human copywriters can provide a very unique perspective, accuracy and writing fashion that it cannot be capable of replicate. Also headings which incorporates "key promoting factors" may want to generally get replaced with more consumer quality ones. Therefore, it's miles advocated to check and edit the replica generated through way of it to make sure its extraordinary and accuracy.

In precis, ChatGPT may be a powerful tool for copywriting webpages, particularly for businesses or those who want to create persuasive and compelling reproduction for their internet internet web sites.

How to Integrate ChatGPT into Your Chatbots

In recent years, chatbots have grow to be an increasingly famous manner for organizations to automate client interactions and decorate customer service. Chatbots use synthetic intelligence (AI) and natural language processing (NLP) to recognize and respond to client queries, imparting rapid and inexperienced customer support.

One way to enhance the effectiveness of chatbots is via way of integrating ChatGPT into the tool. It can enhance the chatbot's functionality to apprehend and reply to consumer queries through supplying extra accurate and natural language responses.

Here is an example of the manner a chatbot can be covered with it:

Suppose we're running our on line T blouse keep and we want to decorate its customer service through the use of enforcing a chatbot. The chatbot can be integrated with ChatGPT to provide herbal language responses to consumer queries. Here's how it may paintings:

1. The chatbot is programmed to recognize and reply to client queries primarily based mostly on key terms and predefined responses.

2. When a consumer enters a question, the chatbot makes use of NLP to apprehend the question and search for a applicable reaction in its database.

3. If the chatbot cannot discover a applicable response in its database, it sends the query to ChatGPT for processing.

four. ChatGPT analyzes the query and generates a herbal language reaction based totally totally on its expertise of the question.

5.   The chatbot gets the response from it and sends it to the patron.

By integrating ChatGPT into the chatbot system, the company can offer extra accurate and natural language responses to client queries, improving the client enjoy and number one satisfaction.

To combine it into your chatbot device, you'll want to have a few technical information in AI and NLP. However, there also are pre-constructed chatbot structures that already have it included, making it less difficult for agencies to installation their chatbots with it. One well-known chatbot platform that lets in integration ChatGPT is Dialogflow. This is beyond the scope of this lecture, however experience loose to analyze it your self. You should even use ChatGPT to help studies it. Now there's an idea!

In stop, integrating ChatGPT into your chatbot tool can beautify the chatbot's ability to recognize and reply to client queries, supplying a greater natural language reaction and improving the customer experience. By the usage of pre-constructed chatbot systems with integration, corporations can effects installation their chatbot with it and provide more price to their customers even as no longer having large technical knowledge.

CHAPTER 9: Ideas For Creating Videos Using ChatGPT and Other AI Tools

Video creation has turn out to be an vital part of content material advertising techniques for masses groups. With the improvement of synthetic intelligence (AI) technology, video introduction has grow to be much less hard, greater green, and further price-powerful. ChatGPT, at the side of special AI device, can be used to create movies which may be appealing, informative, and attractive to the goal market.

Here are some examples of ways AI and ChatGPT may be utilized in video introduction:

1. Video modifying: AI-powered video improving software program will have a look at video images, stumble upon faces, and use algorithms to create cuts and transitions that wholesome the temper

and tone of the video. This saves time and decreases the want for manual improving.

2. Voiceovers: It can be used to generate remarkable voiceovers for movement images. By feeding the script into ChatGPT, it is able to examine the text and generate a voiceover that sounds herbal and attractive.

3. Captioning and subtitling: It may be used to mechanically generate captions and subtitles for films. This makes the video extra available to a far broader target marketplace, which includes individuals who are deaf or tough of listening to.

4. Video content introduction: It can be used to generate thoughts and ideas for video content. By analyzing are searching out trends and social media conversations, it is able to discover famous subjects and generate content material cloth ideas

which is probably applicable to the target audience.

5. Personalization: AI system can be used to personalize video content to make it extra engaging to the viewer. For example, AI can examine the viewer's browsing data, demographics, and special information to create customized hints or tailor-made content material.

6. Visual outcomes: AI may be used to characteristic visible effects to films, together with virtual backgrounds, computer pix, or animations. This enhances the seen appeal of the video and makes it greater attractive to the viewer.

Going into this difficulty count number in depth is outdoor the scope of this training. However, with the aid of using incorporating AI and ChatGPT into video creation, corporations can create excellent movement pics extra effectively and charge-correctly. It additionally allows corporations to tailor their movies to their audience and create extra enticing content. However, it's miles crucial to be conscious that AI and ChatGPT are not an alternative preference to human creativity and understanding. These device are supposed to decorate the video introduction system, now not update it totally.

How to Create Images with Dall-E-2

Visuals have end up a essential detail in hundreds of forms of communique, in particular in virtual advertising. Images no longer only help to deliver records speedy, however moreover they devise an emotional connection with the target market. However, it can be hard to locate an appropriate picture that fits your specific message. That's wherein OpenAI DALL-E 2 is to be had in - it allows you to create custom pictures which may be particular and tailor-made on your dreams.

OpenAI DALL-E 2 is an AI model that generates pix from textual enter. It's the second new release of the DALL-E version, which changed into launched by manner of OpenAI in early 2021. It can generate a tremendous type of photographs, from regular devices to surreal scenes and summary thoughts. The photos it creates are not just popular pix, however custom-made visuals that in shape your precise requirements.

Here's how you could use it to create custom snap shots:

1.   Identify the message: The first step is to select out out the message you want to supply. This will be some thing from selling a product to illustrating a concept.

2.   Write a textual input: Once you have got were given a message, the following

step is to put in writing down a textual input that describes what you want to create. The enter have to be as descriptive as feasible, as the first rate of the photograph will rely upon the readability of the textual input.

3. Submit the input: Once you've got written the textual enter, you could positioned up it to DALL-E 2. The AI model will then generate a custom photograph based in your input.

4. Refine and edit the picture: Once the photo is generated, you could refine and edit it to wholesome your specific necessities. You can alter the coloration, period, and different seen elements to create the suitable picture that conveys your message correctly.

Click Start growing with DALL-E, have a look at the gadget and you could then see the subsequent page in which youcan

Type in question: "Generate a photo of a tshirt for Tshirt logo referred to as "G shirts" It have to be excessive first-class and modern day"

As you can see a number of pix have been created for our T blouse logo called "G Shirts". We have specific that the T Shirts are excessive high-quality and modern.

We can alter the question to create the form of photo we desire. Then we can debate with management, a designer or a whole group of creatives to use the thoughts a start line for the finished product.

Here are a few examples of methods DALL-E 2 can be used in high-quality industries:

1. Marketing and advertising: It may be used to create custom pictures for marketing and advertising and marketing and marketing campaigns. By generating

images which might be unique to the services or products, corporations can create visuals that resonate with their audience.

2. Education: It may be used to create visuals that assist to illustrate complicated thoughts in schooling. By generating custom photos that during form the trouble depend, teachers can create greater engaging content for their university college students.

3. Art and layout: It can be used to create precise and surreal photographs which is probably no longer viable to create via conventional method. Artists and architects can use It to discover new innovative possibilities and push the boundaries in their craft.

In end, OpenAI DALL-E 2 is a powerful tool for developing custom snap shots that healthful your specific necessities. It allows you to create visuals which is probably tailored on your message, supporting to interact and resonate collectively with your target audience. With the help of AI and device learning, companies and creators can unfastened up new contemporary possibilities and create visuals that stand out in a crowded digital landscape.

CHAPTER 10: Python Programming With ChatGPT

ChatGPT hit the headlines at the same time as the sector discovered out it could each write programming code and help in coding responsibilities. One capability software program of the usage of it for coding is to allow non-technical customers to create packages using herbal language in desire to code. It can be used to generate natural language descriptions of the code, or to assist in writing code based mostly on inputs from non-technical clients.

Another capability software of it for coding is probably within the area of code generation and of completion. It might be professional on a huge corpus of code to take a look at common coding styles and generate code snippets based totally on herbal language descriptions of the popular code. For example, a purchaser may additionally need to enter a natural language description of a feature they want to create, and it could generate the corresponding code snippet.

As Python is a famous programming language used for writing code. Let us write a "Hello, World!" software program software in Python:

Type in question: "the manner to write down "hey global" program in python"

However we've just scratched the surface. It can write more complicated applications. Let's write a python software program on the manner to create a desk of all of the t shirts we're promoting. We can use this desk to save information of the differing types and sizes of t shirts.

Type in question: "write a python software an super manner to create a table of t shirts with 20 strains in it. The t blouse table shops the t shirt style plus the quantity of small , medium and large t shirts. The application should have a look at and output the first 10 strains of the table"

As a Python programmer myself. I can verify that the above software program works wonderful, no matter the reality that it could and need to be improved.

Apart from this, it could additionally be used to assist in code evaluation and debugging duties. It may be skilled to investigate code and generate natural language descriptions of capacity problems, or to signify viable solutions to coding troubles based completely mostly on herbal language inputs.

Overall, while ChatGPT isn't specially designed for coding responsibilities, it has the functionality to be useful in advantageous programs associated with herbal language programming and code generation/crowning glory, similarly to in supporting with code assessment and debugging obligations.

How to Make Money Online With ChatGPT

Using ChatGPT to make cash may be powerful as it offers a completely particular and precious abilities set that can be leveraged to provide plenty of offerings. It is an AI language version that could generate human-like responses, examine text, and perform severa language-associated obligations. As such, it may be used to offer a huge sort of offerings, which include:

1. Writing offerings: It can be used to install writing articles, blog posts, social media content material, and amazing kinds of content material material. Its ability to generate human-like responses and look at text can assist produce

splendid content cloth fabric that engages and informs the target marketplace.

2. Editing and proofreading services: It can be used to edit and proofread textual content, ensuring that it's miles grammatically accurate and mistakes-loose. Its language processing talents can help understand and correct mistakes that might be unnoticed with the aid of manner of human editors.

three. Translation offerings: It can be used to translate text from one language to each distinctive. Its language processing skills can assist make sure correct translations and decorate translation general overall performance.

4. Transcription services: It may be used to transcribe audio and video recordings into text. Its ability to generate human-like responses and have a look at textual

content can assist produce accurate and reliable transcripts.

five. Voiceover services: It may be used to generate human-like voiceovers for movies, podcasts, and different varieties of content material. Its language processing talents can help produce top notch voiceovers that sound natural and tasty.

In addition, the usage of ChatGPT to make coins can provide a aggressive advantage because of the reality it is a alternatively new era that is not extensively to be had. As such, there may be a high demand for services that use it, and those who can offer those services can command better fees.

Where Can I Make Money With ChatGPT?

There are numerous systems that you may use to make coins with ChatGPT, collectively with:

1.   Fiverr: Fiverr is an internet marketplace wherein freelancers can provide pretty some services, which incorporates writing, enhancing, translation, transcription, and voiceover offerings using ChatGPT. As a freelancer, you could create a profile on Fiverr, show off your abilities, set your fees, and bid on relevant jobs.

2.   Upwork: Upwork is a well-known platform that connects freelancers with customers seeking out severa offerings, such as writing, improving, translation, transcription, and voiceover offerings using ChatGPT. As a freelancer, you may create a profile on Upwork, take a look at for relevant jobs, and artwork with customers from round the area.

3.   Freelancer: Freelancer is an internet platform that connects freelancers with clients searching out severa offerings, which includes writing, improving,

translation, transcription, and voiceover services the use of ChatGPT. As a freelancer, you can create a profile on Freelancer, bid on relevant jobs, and paintings with clients from round the area.

four. PeoplePerHour: PeoplePerHour is a platform that connects freelancers with clients searching out diverse services, which incorporates writing, improving, translation, transcription, and voiceover offerings using ChatGPT. As a freelancer, you may create a profile on PeoplePerHour, bid on relevant jobs, and art work with clients from around the location.

five. Guru: Guru is a web platform that connects freelancers with customers searching out numerous services, along side writing, improving, translation, transcription, and voiceover services the use of ChatGPT. As a freelancer, you can create a profile on Guru, bid on applicable jobs, and art work with clients from spherical the area.

It's critical to have a look at that the selection for for ChatGPT-associated services might also furthermore variety relying on the platform and the unique provider presented. Some structures may moreover furthermore have extra customers looking for those services than others, and a few services may be greater in-demand than others. Therefore, it is a great idea to investigate every platform and look at which of them may be the high-quality healthful for your competencies and desires.

How Can I Make Money With ChatGPT On Fiverr?

Let's take Fiverr for example. In order to apply ChatGPT To make cash on Fiverr right here's what to do:

1. Create a Fiverr account: Sign up for a Fiverr account and fill out your profile collectively with your capabilities, enjoy, and portfolio samples. Make advantageous your profile is whole, professional, and appealing to ability customers.

2. Define your services: Decide what services you need to provide based totally in your AI language version capabilities. For instance, you can offer writing offerings for articles, blog posts, or social media content. You can also provide enhancing, proofreading, or translation services for texts in remarkable languages. You may also additionally even provide voiceover or transcription offerings using your AI language version.

three. Set your prices: Determine how lots you need to rate in your services. Consider your enjoy, capabilities, and the decision for in your offerings. Research what unique freelancers are charging for similar offerings and set your expenses therefore.

4. Promote your services: Once your services are defined and your fees are set, start selling your services on Fiverr. Use relevant key terms for your gig titles and descriptions to reason them to more discoverable to potential customers. Share your gigs on social media or other on-line systems to reach a far broader goal market.

five. Deliver tremendous paintings: Once you start receiving orders, make sure to deliver amazing paintings on time. Communicate in reality together together with your customers and ask for comments to improve your services. Providing notable customer support will can help you build a tremendous reputation on Fiverr and trap extra customers.

Remember that being worthwhile on Fiverr calls for self-control, hard artwork, and staying electricity. It may additionally take the time to assemble a sturdy popularity and lure a regular go with the waft of customers, but with staying power and excellent art work, you could gain your dreams.

Overall, the usage of ChatGPT to make coins can be a effective device especially in case you use the talents and enjoy on this e-book. By leveraging the particular skills of ChatGPT, people can offer a variety of wonderful services that could assist them succeed in the swiftly evolving digital economic device. You may be capable of explode your productiveness, help others reach their goals and make extra cash on line!

Challenges and Limitations Of ChatGPT

ChatGPT, the herbal language processing (NLP) model advanced with the aid of OpenAI, has received exquisite popularity due to its capability to generate human-like text. However, like every different era, it has its limitations. In this article, we are able to discover some of the essential issue limitations of it and why it's miles essential to be aware about them.

Bias and Inaccuracies

One of the precept boundaries of ChatGPT is its ability for bias and inaccuracies in the textual content it generates. This is because of the reality the model is knowledgeable on massive datasets of human-generated textual content, that could embody biased and misguided information. It can also generate textual content that perpetuates unstable stereotypes or offensive language. It's critical to keep in mind that it isn't a opportunity for important questioning and evaluation, and its output ought to constantly be evaluated for accuracy and bias.

Lack of Contextual Understanding

While it's miles able to generating textual content that appears to be coherent and natural or maybe has some context, it won't necessarily have a "deep" understanding of context. This way that it is able to generate textual content that does not make enjoy within the context of the conversation or may be off-topic. It's vital to make sure that it is informed on a dataset it's miles applicable to the context of the conversation it's miles being carried out in.

Limited Understanding of Nuance and Emotion

It can generate text it really is emotionally charged, but it has a confined data of nuance and emotion. This technique that it can now not constantly be capable of appropriately deliver the meant emotion or tone of the textual content. It's crucial to hold this trouble in mind at the equal time as the usage of It for obligations that require a deep knowledge of emotion, which embody customer service or intellectual health packages. This is likewise why human evaluation and rewriting of the output is usually recommended.

Resource-Intensive

It is a complex system getting to know version that requires huge computing assets to run. This way that it couldn't be viable for some packages or use cases, especially human beings with restricted sources or budget. You may moreover word which you can not get admission to the ChatGPT net interface for the cause that website is in constant use and

OpenAI's server sources can be overloaded.

Dependence on Data Quality

The first-rate of the records used to teach it is a vital difficulty in its normal standard overall performance. It's Garbage In Garbage Out. Therefore as noted if the schooling records is biased, faulty, or incomplete, it's miles output can be in addition improper. It's crucial to do your private research and don't forget that we're the those who make the choices. The AI must only be used as a tool so we will do our incredible art work and assist others.

Chapter 11: Why is ChatGPT Imrtnt?

One of the maximum essential tendencies in synthetic intelligence in present day years has been ChatGPT, a huge language version created through way of OpenAI. ChatGPT has the functionality to convert how we've got got interaction with era due to its capability to recognize and bring human-like language, allowing us to talk extra efficiently, correctly, and intuitively.

Natural Language Processing

The area of natural language processing (NLP) is clearly one among ChatGPT's maximum essential applications. The NLP subfield makes a speciality of using herbal language in communique amongst machines and those. With ChatGPT, programmers can assemble sensible chatbots and virtual assistants that could interpret and respond to actual-time natural language inquiries.

This has large implications for numerous industries, which embody healthcare, finance, customer support, and training. In the healthcare industry, ChatGPT, for instance, may be used to assess affected character information and offer individualized treatment recommendations. In finance, it is able to assist clients navigate complicated monetary services and products.

Language Translation

Language translation is some other crucial vicinity wherein ChatGPT may be used. With its potential to apprehend and generate textual content in a couple of languages, ChatGPT has the functionality to permit seamless conversation at some stage in language limitations. This have to have sizeable implications for worldwide commercial agency, excursion, and worldwide family members, further to for those who talk a couple of languages or who're studying a brand new language.

ChatGPT has already been used to growth translation device that may translate textual content among a couple of languages in actual-time, making it less tough for humans to talk with every incredible irrespective of their language.

Content Creation

ChatGPT's capacity to generate human-like language has giant implications for content creation. Developers can produce content extra rapid and effectively with ChatGPT, giving them greater time for different crucial obligations. ChatGPT can also generate optimized content material cloth for unique audiences or structures, collectively with social media or search engines like google and yahoo like google and yahoo.

ChatGPT also can be used to generate headlines, summaries, and captions which is probably more likely to have interaction readers or traffic. It can also be used to generate product descriptions, weblog posts, and particular content optimized for are searching for engine scores, developing the visibility of groups and agencies on-line.

Education

The area of education is considered one in each of ChatGPT's maximum massive applications. With its potential to understand and generate language similar to that of humans, ChatGPT can be used to create custom designed studying studies that adapt to the desires and abilties of individual novices. This have to appreciably beautify educational outcomes and decrease the achievement hollow.

For example, ChatGPT can be used to create interactive getting to know research that adapt to the tempo and fashion of person novices. It also can offer personalised feedback and help, helping novices apprehend regions wherein they need to enhance and supplying assets and guidance to assist them prevail.

Research

Finally, ChatGPT has splendid implications for research at some point of severa fields. It can recognize and bring language that is much like that of people., ChatGPT may be used to investigate huge quantities of text facts greater rapid and accurately than human researchers.

ChatGPT may be used to research social media data to come to be aware of developments and styles in public opinion or to analyze medical literature to discover connections amongst one in all a kind areas of research. In addition, ChatGPT can assist with records annotation and special time-consuming chores for human researchers, saving up time for extra crucial art work. ChatGPT is important because it has the capacity to exchange how we talk with era and each other sincerely.

How Does ChatGPT Work?

ChatGPT makes use of deep mastering techniques to reply to text-primarily based absolutely enter that resembles human speech. The version is primarily based on a form of neural network called a Transformer shape, which excels at processing sequential records, like text. To understand how ChatGPT works, it's far beneficial to recognize how deep gaining knowledge of works more broadly. At a excessive diploma, deep studying involves training a neural community on a huge dataset to research styles and institutions in the data. The neural network includes layers of interconnected nodes, or neurons, that manner records in a hierarchical style. Each layer of the network builds upon the previous layer, allowing the community to observe more and more complicated representations of the statistics.

In the case of language fashions like ChatGPT, the motive is to educate the version on a big corpus of the text just so it could learn how to understand and generate natural language. During training, the model is fed sequences of text and learns to are awaiting the following phrase in the series. For instance, if the model is given the collection "The cat sat on the ___," it ought to are watching for the word "mat" with a fantastically low hazard thinking about that word does no longer make experience inside the context of the sentence.

To make those predictions, the model uses a way called self-attention; this allows it to weigh the significance of diverse enter collection components even as growing a prediction. This is particularly essential in language modeling, wherein the context of the enter series is important for understanding its which means. After the model has been skilled, it is able to be used to create text thru the use of "priming" it with a primary set of inputs after which generating the following terms inside the collection the use of the opportunities it has located out. To produce a whole response, this technique is iterated upon.

How ChatGPT is Trained

ChatGPT is a language version for synthetic intelligence which could answer textual content-primarily based without a doubt questions in a way that seems like a human. The development of ChatGPT worried schooling the version on a large dataset of textual content-based facts the use of a way referred to as unsupervised gaining knowledge of. We will communicate how ChatGPT modified into expert, collectively with the dataset, training procedure, and strategies and strategies used to refine the model.

1. Dataset Used for Training

The dataset used to teach ChatGPT is called the Common Crawl, a huge collection of net pages crawled and indexed through using search engines. The Common Crawl includes billions of net pages and gives a various and comprehensive deliver of text-based totally certainly records for schooling the version.

The Common Crawl dataset consists of text in various languages, which allowed the group at OpenAI to educate ChatGPT on a huge sort of linguistic styles and structures. This helped enhance the model's capability to generate coherent and applicable responses to the given spark off, no matter the language used.

2. Training Process

The schooling process for ChatGPT involved numerous steps, which encompass facts preprocessing, model initialization, and terrific-tuning. The method took several weeks to complete and involved on foot the model on a big community of GPUs.

3. Data Preprocessing

The first step in the schooling method concerned preprocessing the Common Crawl dataset to put off any inappropriate or redundant records. This blanketed putting off markup language, which includes HTML tags, and filtering out any non-textual records, consisting of photographs or movies.

The crew at OpenAI moreover implemented severa preprocessing techniques to enhance the pleasant of the data used for schooling. For example, they used a way known as byte pair encoding, which includes breaking down terms into smaller subwords to decorate the version's functionality to recognize uncommon or occasionally used phrases.

four. Model Initialization

Once the dataset have become preprocessed, the group initialized the model the use of a way called unsupervised studying. This involved schooling the model on the Common Crawl dataset without express guidance or feedback. This allowed the version to check on its private via identifying patterns and systems inside the information that allowed it to make predictions approximately new statistics.

Unsupervised studying consists of schooling the version to expect the subsequent phrase in a string of textual content given the string's preceding phrases. This allowed the model to discover ways to recognize and generate patterns and structures in human language, which encompass grammar, syntax, and semantics.

5. Fine-Tuning

After the model changed into initialized the use of unsupervised mastering, the team at OpenAI extremely good-tuned the version on a smaller dataset of text-primarily based totally information. This helped beautify the model's functionality to generate responses particular to the given assignment or utility.

The super-tuning technique involved adjusting the parameters of the model to optimize its performance for a particular venture or software. This protected adjusting the getting to know price, the batch length, and distinct hyperparameters influencing the education process.

The Features of ChatGPT

ChatGPT is a contemporary natural language processing version with the capability to recognize and react to natural language input in a manner that cautiously resembles human conversation. ChatGPT is based totally definitely totally on a shape of synthetic neural network referred to as a transformer, which permits it to manner big portions of information and take a look at complicated patterns in natural language.

1. Language Understanding

One of the primary capabilities of ChatGPT is its functionality to interpret and examine enter in natural language. This approach that ChatGPT can examine the that means of sentences, discover applicable data, and respond efficiently.

ChatGPT achieves this through a device called language modeling, wherein it learns to are searching in advance to the opportunity of a phrase or collection of phrases based totally on the context wherein they seem. This permits ChatGPT to generate responses that aren't best grammatically correct however moreover semantically coherent.

2. Context Awareness

Another important characteristic of ChatGPT is its context reputation. ChatGPT is designed to understand the context wherein a verbal exchange is taking vicinity, which consist of the challenge being cited, the speaker's intentions, and the speaker's preceding statements. As a result, ChatGPT may additionally additionally provide replies which might be relevant and suitable for the modern-day discourse.

three. Naturalness

ChatGPT is likewise designed to generate responses that sound natural and human-like. This is finished through a aggregate of factors, at the side of its functionality to understand the nuances of herbal language, its functionality to generate responses which are semantically coherent, and its use of a large database of actual-global conversations to take a look at from.

four. Adaptability

Another critical characteristic of ChatGPT is its adaptability. ChatGPT is designed to research and adapt to new contexts and situations over the years. This way that because it approaches greater facts and encounters new sorts of conversations, it could enhance its regularly occurring performance and generate greater correct and applicable responses.

5. Multilingualism

ChatGPT is likewise designed to be multilingual, due to this it could apprehend and respond to enter in multiple languages. This is finished through a way known as skip- lingual switch mastering, wherein ChatGPT uses its facts of one language to research and adapt to different languages.

6. Consistency

ChatGPT is created to generate replies which can be consistent with beyond statements and actions. This way that if someone asks ChatGPT a question after which follows up with greater questions or statements, ChatGPT will keep in mind the preceding communique and generate consistent responses.

7. Flexibility

Finally, ChatGPT is designed to be bendy and adaptable to important use times and programs. This method that it is able to be customized and optimized for precise obligations, which embody customer support or content technology, and may be covered with extraordinary era and systems to enhance its competencies. Overall, the competencies of ChatGPT make a contribution to its ordinary overall performance and abilties as a natural language processing model.

Its ability to interpret and analyze enter in herbal language, its context awareness, naturalness, adaptability, multilingualism, consistency, and flexibility all make a contribution to its capacity to generate applicable, accurate, and human-like responses to a vast shape of conversational inputs. As such, ChatGPT has the capability to revolutionize the way we've interaction with era and beautify our lives in lots of methods.

Different Version and length of ChatGPT and Their Intended makes use of

ChatGPT, or Generative Pre-professional Transformer, was created with the aid of the usage of OpenAI and is expert to generate textual content that looks like human phrases. The actual ChatGPT version modified into released in 2019, and because then, there had been numerous variations and sizes of ChatGPT models superior for special features.

The specific ChatGPT version, additionally known as ChatGPT-1, grow to be released in June 2019.

It grow to be created the use of a widespread body of text records and became capable of producing coherent and fluent textual content. ChatGPT-1 had 117 million parameters and became educated on a dataset of 40GB of textual content information.

The primary purpose of ChatGPT-1 have turn out to be to carry out language-producing responsibilities such as textual content very last contact, summarization, and translation. It end up furthermore able to answering questions, generating captions, or even writing poetry. ChatGPT-1 speedy have emerge as well-known and turn out to be extensively used within the herbal language processing (NLP) community.

ChatGPT-2, the second model of the ChatGPT version, modified into launched in February 2019. It modified into a miles massive and extra effective version than ChatGPT-1, with 1.Five billion parameters. ChatGPT-2 end up knowledgeable on a dataset of 40GB of text records, which turned into the identical dataset used to educate ChatGPT-1.

ChatGPT-2 come to be designed for various language generation duties, in conjunction with textual content very last touch, summarization, translation, or perhaps writing articles and recollections. It could also generate first-rate poetry or maybe create faux information articles which have been indistinguishable from actual records articles.

However, short after its launch, OpenAI determined now not to release the overall version of ChatGPT-2 because of troubles about the capability misuse of the model for generating fake facts and one-of-a-kind malicious capabilities.

ChatGPT-3 is the zero.33 and most powerful model of the ChatGPT model. It have become launched in June 2020. It is one in every of the maximum crucial language fashions ever built, with a hundred 75 billion parameters. ChatGPT-3 became knowledgeable on a big dataset of 45TB of text statistics, it's far equal to the textual content contained in masses of books.

ChatGPT-3 changed into designed for severa language responsibilities, which include textual content final touch, summarization, translation, or maybe programming. It have become moreover able to producing notable poetry, growing fake information articles, or perhaps producing new textual content primarily based on a given prompt.

ChatGPT-3 fast gained recognition and became utilized in diverse packages, which consist of chatbots, digital assistants, or even innovative writing equipment. However, due to its huge size and excessive computational necessities, ChatGPT-3 changed into now not on hand to most customers.

ChatGPT-Neo is a sequence of models evolved by means of using manner of EleutherAI, an open-supply business enterprise that goals to create available AI fashions. The ChatGPT-Neo models are knowledgeable using the same architecture and dataset because the actual ChatGPT fashions but with smaller sizes.

The smallest ChatGPT-Neo model has most effective one hundred twenty five million parameters, it genuinely is just like the dimensions of ChatGPT-1. The largest ChatGPT-Neo model has 2.7 billion parameters, that could be a exquisite deal smaller than ChatGPT-2 but but able to producing terrific text.

ChatGPT-Neo have become designed to be accessible to developers and researchers who do now not have get proper of entry to to huge quantities of computing strength. The fashions are to be had for free and may be run on a private pc.

Chapter 12: Technical Requirements for Implementing ChatGPT

ChatGPT language version can comprehend spoken language and bring replies that resemble those of someone. To positioned into effect ChatGPT, numerous technical necessities need to be considered.

1. Computing Power

The first technical requirement for implementing ChatGPT is computing power. The length and complexity of the model require massive computing resources to educate and run. The version requires a big quantity of reminiscence and processing energy to characteristic efficiently. Thus, powerful computers or servers equipped with GPUs are desired for the implementation of ChatGPT.

2. Data

The second technical requirement for enforcing ChatGPT is data. ChatGPT requires a huge quantity of exquisite training statistics to analyze and apprehend human language. This statistics can be obtained from numerous assets which includes social media, web net websites, and books. The records need to be pre-processed and wiped clean in advance than getting used to educate the version. Data cleaning is the manner of removing any useless facts, collectively with duplicate or irrelevant information, from the dataset.

3. Natural Language Processing

The 0.33 technical requirement for implementing ChatGPT is herbal language processing (NLP). ChatGPT makes use of NLP techniques to apprehend human language and generate human-like responses.

NLP includes numerous responsibilities, together with detail-of-speech tagging, named entity recognition, and sentiment analysis. These duties are critical to recognize the context of a sentence and generate a large reaction.

four. Deep Learning Framework

The fourth technical requirement for implementing ChatGPT is a deep studying framework. Deep reading frameworks are software libraries that allow the implementation of complicated neural network fashions. The maximum famous deep studying frameworks are TensorFlow, PyTorch, and Keras. These frameworks provide a fixed of gadget for constructing, schooling, and comparing neural network fashions.

5. Pre-Trained Model

The fifth technical requirement for enforcing ChatGPT is a pre-professional model. OpenAI has released numerous pre-knowledgeable versions of ChatGPT, which include GPT-2 and GPT-3, that may be used for severa natural language processing responsibilities. These pre-skilled models have already determined out from a large corpus of text and can generate incredible responses to consumer queries.

6. API

The 6th technical requirement for implementing ChatGPT is an API. An API, or utility programming interface, is a tough and rapid of protocols that lets in specific software software software packages to talk with each different.

ChatGPT may be included with severa packages consisting of chatbots, voice assistants, and customer service structures. The API gives a simple interface for the ones applications to talk with the ChatGPT version.

7. Deployment Infrastructure

The seventh technical requirement for implementing ChatGPT is deployment infrastructure. The deployment infrastructure is the environment wherein the ChatGPT version runs.

This infrastructure ought to be scalable and fault-tolerant to ensure that the model can deal with a huge sort of requests and keep excessive availability. Cloud-primarily based absolutely infrastructure consisting of Amazon Web Services (AWS) or Microsoft Azure may be used for deployment.

eight. Security

The eighth technical requirement for imposing ChatGPT is protection. Security is an important factor of any software program program tool, and ChatGPT is not any exception. ChatGPT must be covered in the direction of capacity protection threats including hacking and unauthorized get right of entry to to purchaser facts. Encryption and solid conversation protocols must be completed to defend person data and make certain privacy.

9. Performance Monitoring

The ninth technical requirement for implementing ChatGPT is performance monitoring. Performance monitoring consists of tracking the overall universal performance of the model and detecting any problems that can upward push up.

Monitoring can be carried out using various gear which consist of log evaluation and real-time tracking systems. Performance monitoring allows to understand and solve any common performance issues that could have an effect at the purchaser experience.

How to use ChatGPT

ChatGPT, a huge language version superior with the aid of OpenAI, has the functionality to recognize and generate human-like language, making it an incredibly effective tool for a huge kind of packages. Let's find out the way to use ChatGPT and provide some pointers and superb practices for buying the most out of this effective tool.

1. Understanding the Basics

Before you could start using ChatGPT, it's far crucial to apprehend the basics of the way the device works. At its middle, ChatGPT is a herbal language processing (NLP) tool that uses deep reading algorithms to understand and generate human-like language.

To use ChatGPT, you honestly input a hard and fast off or query, and the device will generate a response primarily based totally on its information of human language. The responses generated with the useful resource of ChatGPT are primarily based on its schooling information, which includes a big amount of text from a giant sort of assets, such as books, articles, and internet web sites.

2. Choosing a Platform

There are a number of one in every of a kind systems and device available for using

ChatGPT, each with its own strengths and weaknesses. Some of the maximum famous structures for the usage of ChatGPT include:

OpenAI's API: OpenAI gives an API that lets in builders to mix ChatGPT into their very non-public applications and offerings.

GPT-three Playground: The GPT-3 Playground is an internet-primarily based completely tool that lets in customers to interact with ChatGPT with none coding required.

Hugging Face: Hugging Face is a platform that offers a big sort of herbal language processing tools, which incorporates access to ChatGPT.

When selecting a platform for the use of ChatGPT, it's far crucial to recall your particular dreams and necessities. For example, if you're a developer seeking out to combine ChatGPT into your very own software program, OpenAI's API can be the exceptional opportunity. If you're a non-technical individual looking for a clean way to interact with ChatGPT, the GPT-three Playground can be a higher healthy.

3. Providing Clear Prompts

To get the most correct and useful responses from ChatGPT, it is vital to offer easy and unique turns on. This manner warding off vague or open-ended questions and as an opportunity supplying specific and nicely-defined turns on.

For instance, in location of asking, "What's the tremendous way to shed kilos?", it really is a indistinct and open-ended question, you may ask, "What are some powerful sporting occasions for burning stomach fat?" it actually is a extra specific and well-described activate.

Providing clear activates allows ChatGPT better apprehend your query's context and reason, permitting it to generate greater accurate and beneficial responses.

4. Understanding Limitations

While ChatGPT is a powerful tool, it's important to recognize its limitations. One of the most essential obstacles of ChatGPT is that it's miles simplest as accurate and dependable due to the fact the schooling data it is been fed. This approach that if the training data includes biases or inaccuracies, ChatGPT may also moreover generate in addition biased or defective responses.

Additionally, ChatGPT may be better and can sometimes generate responses which may be nonsensical or irrelevant. It's important to examine the responses generated via ChatGPT and use your very personal judgment to determine whether or not or no longer or no longer they may be accurate and appropriate.

5. Incorporating Feedback

One of the most effective approaches to decorate the accuracy and value of ChatGPT is to include remarks into the education statistics. This method reviewing the responses generated through ChatGPT and presenting remarks to help enhance the accuracy and relevance of future responses.

For example, if ChatGPT generates an erroneous or beside the factor reaction, you can offer comments indicating that the reaction was incorrect or offensive. This remarks can then be included into the training statistics, supporting to enhance the accuracy and relevance of future responses.

The limitations of ChatGPT

ChatGPT is an excellent instance of an Artificial Intelligence-primarily based Natural Language Processing (NLP) system advanced through manner of way of OpenAI. It is a sophisticated language model that makes use of deep mastering techniques to understand and approach human language, generate textual content, solution questions, and interact in conversations. However, like a few other era, ChatGPT moreover has positive boundaries that have an impact on its ordinary standard performance and accuracy.

Lack of Common Sense

Lack of not unusual revel in is one in every of ChatGPT's predominant drawbacks. While the model is proper at generating textual content based totally on styles within the statistics, it turn out to be informed on and lacks the capability to reason and recognize the sector like humans do. For example, ChatGPT may moreover moreover fail to recognize jokes or sarcasm, because it does no longer have the not unusual feel to interpret the tone or context of a announcement. This lack of common revel in can result in awkward or inappropriate responses.

Biases in Training Data

Another disadvantage of ChatGPT is the biases in its training data. The version is professional on huge quantities of text facts from the internet, which means that that it is able to reflect the biases and prejudices that exist in our society. For example, if the schooling data includes more textual content from one precise demographic enterprise, the version also can produce biased responses within the direction of that employer. Similarly, if the facts consists of horrific stereotypes approximately positive agencies of humans, ChatGPT can also additionally perpetuate the ones stereotypes in its responses.

Inability to Learn from Feedback

ChatGPT is a pre-skilled language version that isn't designed to learn from comments in actual time. This approach that if someone offers remarks on a response generated with the useful resource of ChatGPT, the version will not be able to contain that remarks to enhance its performance within the destiny. This loss of a feedback loop can restriction the model's capacity to investigate and adapt to new facts and contexts.

Limited Domain Knowledge

Another difficulty of ChatGPT is its restrained location know-how. The model is expert on a giant style of text facts from severa domain names, however it could no longer have specialised information in precise regions. For instance, ChatGPT might not have enough understand-the way to provide a significant reaction if a customer asks a question approximately a selected clinical concept. This can be a sizable hassle for customers who're seeking out more in-depth records on unique topics.

Lack of Emotional Intelligence

ChatGPT is likewise constrained in its ability to apprehend and respond to feelings. While the model can apprehend some emotional cues from the text, it can not be capable of interpret complicated emotional states like empathy or compassion. This can limit the model's functionality to provide emotional assist or engage in empathetic conversations with clients who are struggling with emotional or intellectual fitness issues.

Chapter 13: Limited Multilingual Capabilities

ChatGPT is expert especially on English language facts, because of this that that its multilingual talents are restrained. While the model can generate textual content in different languages, its ordinary performance in languages aside from English may not be as accurate or fluent. This may be a obstacle for customers who speak languages aside from English and are searching out a greater seamless conversational revel in.

Risk of Misinformation

Another hassle of ChatGPT is the danger of manufacturing wrong information. As the model is knowledgeable on a large quantity of textual content data from the internet, it may generate responses which is probably factually incorrect or primarily based totally mostly on fake information. This can be a huge trouble for users who depend upon ChatGPT for records and advice.

Limited Contextual Understanding

Lastly, ChatGPT has a constrained know-how of the context. While the model can generate textual content based totally on patterns in the statistics, it was professional on, and it is able to no longer normally be able to understand the overall context of someone's question or declaration.

Potential Impact of ChatGPT on employment and Society

ChatGPT is a current-day natural language processing model developed with the beneficial resource of OpenAI. It has the functionality to apprehend and reply to natural language input in a way that closely mimics human communique. Since its release in 2020, ChatGPT has been notably determined in severa programs, which consist of chatbots, language translation, and content material generation. While ChatGPT has the capability to revolutionize many industries, it additionally will increase questions on its effect on employment and society.

First, allow's maintain in thoughts the effect of ChatGPT on employment. ChatGPT has the capability to automate many jobs that currently require human intervention. For example, customer service jobs that solution smooth questions or offer records can be automated the use of ChatGPT. Similarly, content cloth introduction jobs, which encompass writing product descriptions or social media posts, can also be automated the usage of ChatGPT. While this will result in terrific cost savings for companies, it is able to additionally bring about challenge loss for human people.

However, it's far crucial to examine that ChatGPT moreover has the potential to create new undertaking possibilities. As more companies undertake ChatGPT for customer support and content material fabric creation, there will be a developing call for for builders, information analysts, and distinct technical professionals who can layout, implement, and optimize ChatGPT systems. Additionally, there can be new possibilities for human employees to provide greater complicated and specialised services that cannot be computerized the use of ChatGPT.

Moreover, ChatGPT can be used to beautify the productiveness and overall performance of cutting-edge jobs. For instance, ChatGPT may be used as a non-public assistant to assist employees manage their schedules, reply to emails, and perform unique regular obligations. This can help personnel attention on more complicated and revolutionary duties that require human enter.

However, the effect of ChatGPT on employment is likely to be erratically allotted at some stage in one among a type industries and procedure types. Some industries and task kinds can be greater susceptible to automation than others.

For instance, jobs that comprise repetitive obligations or routine information processing are more likely to be computerized using ChatGPT than jobs that require creativity or emotional intelligence. This need to exacerbate gift inequalities in the hard paintings market, with personnel in a few industries and undertaking kinds being disproportionately laid low with automation.

Next, allow's don't forget the impact of ChatGPT on society as an entire. ChatGPT has the capability to beautify get right of entry to to records and services for individuals with language obstacles or disabilities.

ChatGPT can be used to provide actual-time language translation offerings for folks who do not communicate the nearby language. Similarly, ChatGPT can be used to offer accessible facts and services for people with seen impairments or precise disabilities.

Moreover, ChatGPT may be used to enhance the performance and effectiveness of public services. For instance, ChatGPT can be used to provide real-time statistics and help for human beings trying to find healthcare or social offerings.

Similarly, ChatGPT may be used to provide customized education and training offerings for people searching for to gather new talents or statistics. However, the massive adoption of ChatGPT moreover increases concerns approximately privateness and records protection.

ChatGPT structures rely upon big portions of records to investigate and beautify over time. This data can include non-public information approximately humans, which encompass their names, addresses, and alternatives. If this statistics is not correctly blanketed, it can be used for malicious capabilities, which include identity theft or fraud.

Moreover, ChatGPT has the capacity to perpetuate gift biases and inequalities in society. ChatGPT structures examine from the information they may be knowledgeable on, and if this information consists of biases or stereotypes, the ChatGPT device may additionally

additionally reproduce those biases in its responses.

Difference Between ChatGPT and a Search Engine

ChatGPT and search engines like google and yahoo are two first rate herbal language processing (NLP) gadget used for one-of-a-type capabilities. While ChatGPT is designed to engage in conversations with customers and provide customized responses, engines like google are regularly used to go looking and retrieve statistics from the internet.

1. Purpose

The primary purpose of ChatGPT is to offer customized responses to customers in natural language. ChatGPT is designed to mimic human-like conversations and engage clients in a lower again-and-forth speak. It is utilized in chatbots, virtual assistants, and awesome conversational AI programs.

On the other hand, the cause of serps is to retrieve data from the net. Search engines use algorithms to move slowly and index net pages and provide customers with applicable outcomes based on their are seeking for queries. Search engines are usually used to discover statistics and answer unique questions.

2. Interactivity

ChatGPT is made to have conversational interactions with users. It can reply to patron queries, ask comply with-up questions, and provide personalised recommendations. ChatGPT also can recall preceding conversations and use that records to provide extra accurate and applicable responses in the destiny.

Search engines, as an alternative, aren't designed for interactive conversations.

While they're able to provide outcomes based on person queries, they do not have interaction in a decrease lower back- and-forth dialogue with customers. Search engines are usually used to retrieve statistics, and customers are expected to sift via the effects to find out what they're searching out.

3. Knowledge base

The information base of ChatGPT is primarily based mostly on the huge quantities of textual content information it's been skilled on. ChatGPT has been educated on various textual content records, which encompass books, articles, and social media posts. This permits it to have a great expertise of numerous topics and mind. ChatGPT can also examine from person interactions and feedback to beautify its responses over time.

Search engines rely on their algorithms to retrieve information from the internet. Complex algorithms are utilized by search engines like google like google like google to transport slowly online index internet sites, and they prioritize results primarily based mostly on several factors, together with relevance, recognition, and authority. Search engines do not have a selected statistics base inside the equal way ChatGPT does, however they have get proper of entry to to a significant amount of information at the internet.

four. Algorithms

ChatGPT uses a natural language processing set of guidelines to apprehend character queries and generate responses. ChatGPT's set of regulations is based totally totally on a deep getting to know version that has been knowledgeable on large portions of text records. The model makes use of a transformer structure that permits it to recognize the context and because of this of person queries.

Search engines use complicated algorithms to move slowly and index internet pages and retrieve records primarily based on man or woman queries. Search engines use severa factors to prioritize results, collectively with relevance, authority, and recognition. Search engines use a mixture of tool getting to know and rule-based completely algorithms to retrieve and rank results based on the ones factors.

ChatGPT and search engines like google and yahoo are splendid NLP tools used for fantastic abilities. While ChatGPT is designed to interact in conversations with clients and offer customized responses, search engines like google and yahoo are on the entire used to go looking and retrieve information from the net. ChatGPT's reason is to engage in interactive conversations, on the equal time as search engines like google are designed to provide effects based totally mostly on consumer queries.

ChatGPT's knowledge base is based totally totally on huge portions of text information, at the same time as engines like google like google like google depend on algorithms to transport slowly and index internet pages. ChatGPT makes use of a natural language processing set of guidelines to apprehend client queries, at the same time as search engines like google like google use a mixture of device studying and rule-primarily based algorithms to retrieve and rank effects.

Benefits of ChatGPT

ChatGPT is a huge language model evolved by means of manner of using OpenAI that uses deep getting to know strategies to generate human-like responses to text enter. It has been used in various packages, which incorporates chatbots, language translation, and content fabric cloth era. The benefits of ChatGPT are severa, and we're capable of discover some of the maximum big blessings of the use of this generation.

Chapter 14: Improved Customer Service

One of the most huge advantages of ChatGPT is its capability to enhance customer service. By integrating a chatbot with ChatGPT, groups can provide their clients instantaneous assist and help 24/7. This approach that clients now not need to appearance beforehand to an agent to end up to be had, which may be annoying and time-ingesting. Additionally, ChatGPT can control a couple of conversations at the equal time, making sure that each one customers get hold of the resource they want in a well timed and efficient way.

Increased Efficiency

ChatGPT may be used to automate a wide style of duties, that could bring about improved overall performance and productivity. For example, it can be used to generate content material cloth fabric for internet websites, social media, and advertising and marketing substances. This way that companies can produce exquisite content material at scale without the want for a dedicated content material organization. Additionally, ChatGPT may be used to automate repetitive responsibilities, including scheduling appointments or sending out reminders, releasing up frame of employees to attention on extra complex and strategic responsibilities.

Cost Savings

By automating obligations and improving customer service, ChatGPT can cause sizable rate financial savings for companies. For instance, thru the usage of a chatbot with Chat GPT, companies can reduce the want for customer service dealers, which can be a significant rate for masses organizations. Additionally, through automating obligations, businesses can lessen the need for staff, that can similarly reduce prices. This may be in particular useful for small and medium-sized businesses, which may not have the belongings to lease a massive group.

Improved Customer Experience

ChatGPT additionally can be used to decorate the patron revel in via providing personalised suggestions and help. By reading patron information, ChatGPT can offer tailor-made suggestions and suggestions based totally totally on a consumer's possibilities and past behavior. This can assist growth customer delight and loyalty, as customers sense they may be receiving personalised interest and aid.

Increased Sales

ChatGPT can also be used to increase income through providing customers with customized pointers and gives. ChatGPT can emerge as aware about possibilities to upsell or bypass-sell services and products through manner of studying client facts and conduct. This can cause increased income and profitability for groups and extended client delight, as clients sense that they are receiving customized hobby and useful resource.

Multilingual Support

ChatGPT also can be used to provide multilingual guide to clients. Using language translation models, ChatGPT can generate responses in a couple of languages, making sure that businesses can guide clients irrespective of their place or language. This can be mainly beneficial for businesses that perform in more than one international locations or regions, as it can assist to improve client satisfaction and decrease language boundaries.

Scalability

ChatGPT is tremendously scalable, which means that that it can be used to aid a big range of clients concurrently. This is in particular important for businesses that revel in spikes in call for, alongside facet at some stage in excursion periods or income activities. By the use of ChatGPT, corporations can ensure that every one customers acquire the help and help they want, even in the course of pinnacle intervals.

Continuous Learning

ChatGPT is continuously gaining knowledge of and improving, that means that it may provide greater correct and relevant responses over time. This is as it uses deep studying strategies to investigate and understand text enter, which allows it to enhance its statistics and generate greater correct responses. This non-save you studying manner that organizations can depend on ChatGPT to offer fantastic help and assistance to their clients, even as purchaser dreams.

The Risks of ChatGPT

As a language version powered by way of manner of superior synthetic intelligence, ChatGPT has showed to be a powerful device for plenty applications. From answering questions and producing textual content to providing language translation or even supporting with scientific diagnoses, ChatGPT has the potential to convert how we engage with technology and each exclusive.

However, like every device, ChatGPT moreover includes with it a variety of functionality risks that need to be taken into consideration and addressed. Let's explore a number of the most first-rate dangers related to ChatGPT and talk techniques to mitigate those risks.

1. Bias and Discrimination

One of the most essential risks connected with ChatGPT is the functionality for bias and discrimination. This danger arises from the truth that ChatGPT is professional on substantial quantities of information from the net, that could incorporate inherent biases that mirror the views and values of society as an entire.

For instance, if ChatGPT is professional on a dataset that consists of discriminatory or biased language closer to wonderful agencies, it could learn how to reflect these biases in its responses. This should bring about ChatGPT offering discriminatory or offensive responses, that could have intense results for individuals and organizations.

To mitigate this threat, it is critical to make sure that the datasets used to teach ChatGPT are severa, consultant, and unfastened from biases. This may be carried out thru cautious choice and curation of datasets and ongoing tracking and assessment of ChatGPT's responses.

2. Misinformation and Fake News

Another exceptional hazard related to ChatGPT is the capability for incorrect records and faux statistics. The capacity of ChatGPT to generate text this is same to human- written text way that it has the capability to be used to unfold fake or misleading records.

For example, ChatGPT is probably carried out to generate fake facts articles, social media posts, or emails that appear to be written through way of actual humans. This need to have serious outcomes for humans and society, specifically if the faux statistics is spread extensively and extensively influences public opinion or decision-making.

To mitigate this chance, it's miles important to make sure ChatGPT is applied effectively and morally. This can be accomplished via careful tracking and evaluation of ChatGPT's responses, as well as via the improvement of algorithms and device that would discover and flag possibly fake or misleading statistics.

three. Privacy and Security

A 0.33 huge hazard associated with ChatGPT is the capability for privateness and safety breaches. ChatGPT's functionality to generate textual content approach that it has the capacity to gather and preserve massive amounts of sensitive information, collectively with private data, economic records, and first rate private statistics.

If this statistics falls into the incorrect hands, it may be used for malicious features, together with identity robbery, fraud, or distinctive kinds of cybercrime. Additionally, ChatGPT's capacity to generate convincing text might be used to trick human beings into sharing their personal records or passwords, most essential to in addition security breaches.

To mitigate this danger, it's far crucial to ensure that ChatGPT is designed with sturdy privateness and protection skills, inclusive of strong encryption, consistent garage protocols, and strict get proper of access to controls. It is also essential to train users about the risks related to sharing sensitive information with ChatGPT and inspire them to apply robust passwords and distinct safety capabilities.

four. Dependence on Technology

A fourth massive threat related to ChatGPT is the capability for humans and society to become overly dependent on generation. ChatGPT's capability to generate textual content and provide answers to complicated questions may lead human beings to rely too heavily in this period in preference to developing their very own crucial questioning and hassle-solving talents. This must have numerous poor effects, including a decline in creativity, innovation, and social interaction.

Where and When to apply ChatGPT

ChatGPT, a strong tool for herbal language processing, has grown in popularity in modern-day years. This AI language version can understand and respond to human language in a way that mimics human verbal exchange. It has been implemented in severa contexts, from customer support to language translation to instructional applications.

Where to use ChatGPT

1. Customer Service

Customer company chatbots are growing in recognition. They can deal with sincere issues, liberating up human customer service specialists to deal with trickier troubles.

Customers can also ask diverse questions about chatbots powered through manner of ChatGPT and get maintain of tailor-made solutions. Customers can quickly get proper of get admission to to them thinking about the reality that they'll be related into net web sites, cellular packages, and chat offerings. Chatbots can help reduce wait times, offer 24/7 help, and boom patron delight.

2. Language Translation

Moreover, ChatGPT allows language translation. It can translate between a couple of languages fast and as it should be. This may be beneficial for agencies that characteristic in a couple of countries, as it is able to assist them talk with customers and clients who talk first rate languages. ChatGPT can be included into internet websites, mobile apps, and messaging structures to offer a actual-time translation.

three. Educational Applications

ChatGPT additionally can be applied in educational packages. It can be used to create interactive mastering environments wherein university college students can ask questions and get hold of without delay feedback. It can also be used to create digital tutors, that could offer custom designed coaching to university college students. Moreover, ChatGPT can be used to boom chatbots that might reply to inquiries from college college students and provide comments on their artwork.

four. Content Creation

ChatGPT can be used to fast and with out difficulty make content material. It can be used to create articles, weblog posts, and product descriptions. Moreover, it can be used to create emails and postings for social media. ChatGPT can help groups hold time and money on content material introduction even as additionally ensuring that the content fabric is brilliant and applicable.

5. Personal Assistants

Personal assistants which can help customers with handling their normal obligations may be made the use of ChatGPT. These personal assistants can be integrated into cellular apps and messaging structures and may help clients time table appointments, set reminders, and control their to-do lists. ChatGPT also may be used to provide personalised hints and tips based on person options.

Chapter 15: When to apply ChatGPT

1. When coping with massive volumes of records

ChatGPT can be used to analyze and interpret large volumes of information rapid and successfully. This may be useful for businesses that collect large quantities of facts, which consist of client feedback, social media mentions, and internet internet web page analytics. ChatGPT can examine this statistics and provide insights that could assist corporations make informed decisions.

2. When there may be a need for actual-time verbal exchange

ChatGPT can offer real-time communique, which can be useful in customer service and special packages. Chatbots powered through ChatGPT can respond to patron queries proper now, imparting 24/7 resource. This can help corporations deliver higher company to their clients and cause them to happier.

three. When there may be a want for customized communique

ChatGPT may be used to provide customized communication. It can analyze person statistics and provide pointers and suggestions based totally on client possibilities. This may be beneficial in instructional packages, in which customized training can help university college students take a look at greater efficiently.

It moreover may be useful in advertising and advertising, wherein customized recommendations can help businesses growth profits.

4. When there may be a need for green content material fabric creation

ChatGPT may be used to speedy and without problems make content. Compared to how extended a human author could want, it could produce first rate content material a ways quicker. Businesses that want to generate good enough content fabric also can additionally locate this useful, together with e-change web sites and social media.

The Future of ChatGPT

As an AI language model, ChatGPT has come an prolonged manner for the reason that its inception in 2020. It has been able to showcase its competencies in various regions, collectively with herbal language processing, language translation, and language generation. As we look in the direction of the destiny, there are several regions in which ChatGPT can keep to conform and beautify, collectively with its ability to recognize human feelings and its ability to mix with other generation.

One of the important thing regions wherein ChatGPT can decorate is in its capacity to recognize human emotions. Currently, ChatGPT is able to reply to person queries and generate text primarily based on the given enter. However, it lacks the ability to understand the emotional context of the enter. For instance, if someone is feeling sad or hectic and expresses those feelings to ChatGPT, it can not be capable of respond in an empathetic or comforting way.

To cope with this quandary, future variations of ChatGPT may be designed to encompass emotional intelligence. This would contain education the model to recognize emotional cues in user enter and generate suitable responses based totally on the emotional context. For instance, if a consumer expresses sadness, ChatGPT need to answer with comforting phrases or offer property for assist.

ChatGPT have to end up a greater powerful device for assisting intellectual fitness and well-being with the useful aid of incorporating emotional intelligence.

Another area in which ChatGPT can keep to adapt is its capability to combine with different technology. ChatGPT operates as a standalone model, producing text responses based on purchaser input. However, it is able to be integrated with different technologies, together with voice reputation, picture reputation, or device getting to know algorithms.

For instance, ChatGPT will be protected with voice popularity technology to allow users to interact with it through voice instructions. This might also need to make it much less complicated for clients to apply ChatGPT hands-unfastened and while typing is impractical, which incorporates whilst the use of or cooking. Additionally, ChatGPT is probably incorporated with photograph popularity technology to permit clients to go into information the use of pictures or movies. This would amplify the forms of inputs that ChatGPT may moreover need to way, making it greater bendy and customer-great.

Another place in which ChatGPT ought to decorate is its ability to generate extra human- like responses. While ChatGPT is able to generating coherent and informative text, its responses can now and again feel robotic or formulaic. This is due to the fact ChatGPT generates responses primarily based totally on statistical styles in big datasets in preference to a actual data of language and context.

To deal with this problem, destiny versions of ChatGPT have to incorporate greater advanced natural languages processing strategies, together with semantic evaluation or neural networks. These strategies could permit ChatGPT to generate responses primarily based on a deeper knowledge of language and context in preference to definitely statistical styles. Additionally, ChatGPT is probably professional on smaller, greater particular datasets to enhance its capability to generate responses in sure domain names, together with healthcare or finance.

Another area wherein ChatGPT need to decorate is its capability to deal with complicated or ambiguous queries. ChatGPT is excellent applicable for answering truthful questions or imparting statistics on precise topics. However, it is able to conflict with greater complicated or ambiguous queries, collectively with the ones concerning multiple layers of inference or nuanced records.

To deal with this downside, destiny versions of ChatGPT can be designed to deal with more complex queries. This must include incorporating greater superior reasoning and inference techniques, collectively with probabilistic reasoning or deep studying. By improving its ability to address complicated queries, ChatGPT might also moreover want to end up a greater valuable tool for obligations which includes choice-making or trouble-solving.

How Can I Profit from ChatGPT?

As an AI language model, ChatGPT is typically designed to offer solutions, tips, and recommendation to its clients. It can assist in numerous regions which includes training, research, corporation, personal improvement, and leisure. However, almost approximately taking advantage of ChatGPT, you could leverage its capabilities to generate profits in severa ways.

Creating Content

ChatGPT may be a incredible device for growing Content that can be monetized in severa tactics. You can use it to generate mind, thought, and insights for weblog posts, articles, and guides. By tapping into its sizeable records base, you could produce immoderate- extraordinary Content this is informative, attractive, and relevant for your target audience.

For example, in case you run a weblog on technology, you can use ChatGPT to investigate and write about rising developments, improvements, and trends within the tech company. You also can use it to reply frequently requested questions, offer professional critiques, and offer tips and tutorials at the way to apply unique equipment and software program application.

Providing Consulting Services

ChatGPT moreover may be a valuable aid for providing consulting services to customers. As an AI language version, it is able to offer insights and answers to complicated troubles in severa industries together with finance, advertising and marketing, healthcare, and crook. By leveraging its abilties, you could offer customized recommendation and tips to clients which can be tailored to their unique desires and goals.

For instance, in case you are a economic consultant, you could use ChatGPT to analyze marketplace traits, perceive investment opportunities, and offer investment recommendation to customers. You can also use it to generate economic fashions, forecast destiny average overall performance, and examine danger and praise tradeoffs.

Similarly, if you are a marketing representative, you could use ChatGPT to investigate and examine purchaser conduct, become aware of aim audiences, and boom marketing and advertising strategies which may be powerful and tasty. You also can use it to optimize internet site content cloth material, design social media campaigns, and create compelling replica and visuals.

Developing Chatbots

Chatbots are laptop applications that could simulate conversations with human customers. They are used in severa industries, consisting of customer support, earnings, and useful resource. By leveraging the talents of ChatGPT, you could expand greater clever, responsive, and human-like chatbots.

If you run an e-trade maintain, you can use ChatGPT to boom a chatbot which could solution consumer queries, provide product tips, and method orders. By automating customer service, you can shop time and resources at the identical time as improving patron pleasure and loyalty.

And in case you run a healthcare corporation, you may use ChatGPT to amplify a chatbot that can offer scientific recommendation, diagnose symptoms, and time table appointments. By leveraging the expertise of ChatGPT, you may create a chatbot that is accurate, reliable, and privy to the goals of patients.

Conducting Research

ChatGPT may be a precious tool for task research in diverse fields which incorporates generation, social sciences, and arts. By leveraging its extensive information base, you can generate new insights, take a look at hypotheses, and discover new ideas that could result in new discoveries and innovations.

For instance, if you are a scientist, you could use ChatGPT to research studies papers, emerge as aware of understanding gaps, and broaden studies questions that could reason new discoveries. You also can use it to analyze statistics, generate hypotheses, and take a look at theories that could motive new insights and breakthroughs.